Systems Thinking Turbulent Wo

CW01023715

Systems Thinking for a Turbulent World will help practitioners in any field of change engage more effectively in transformative innovation. Such innovation addresses the paradigm shift needed to meet the diverse unfolding global challenges facing us today, often summed up as the Anthropocene.

Fragmentation of local and global societies is escalating, and this is aggravating vicious cycles. To heal the rifts, we need to reintroduce the human element into our understandings – whether the context is civic or scientific – and strengthen truth-seeking in decision-making. Aided by appropriate concepts and methods, this healing will enable a switch from reaction to anticipation, even in the face of discontinuous change and high uncertainty. The outcome is to privilege the positive human skills for collaborative navigation through uncertainty over the disjointed rationality of mechanism and artificial intelligence, which increasingly alienates us.

The reader in search of new ways of thinking will be introduced to concepts new to systems thinking that integrate systems thinking and futures thinking. The concept of anticipatory present moment (APM) serves as a basis for learning the cognitive skills that better enable navigation through turbulent times. A key personal and team practice is participative repatterning, which is the basis for transformative innovation. This practice is aided by new methods of visual facilitation.

The reader is guided through the unfolding of the ideas and practices with a narrative based on the metaphor of search portrayed in the tradition of ox herding, found in traditional Far Eastern consciousness practice.

Anthony Hodgson is currently a trustee and research director of H3Uni – A University for the Third Horizon, a research fellow at the University of Dundee, director of Decision Integrity Limited and a founding member of the International Futures Forum. He has a BSc in chemistry from Imperial College London and PhD in systems science from the University of Hull, Centre for Systems Studies. He has over 30 years of experience as a consultant facilitator in strategy and foresight.

Systems Thinking

Series editor:
Gerald Midgley
University of Hull, UK

Systems Thinking theory and practice is gaining ground in the worlds of social policy and management.

The Routledge *Systems Thinking* series is designed to make this complex subject as easy for busy practitioners and researchers to understand as possible. It provides range of reference books, textbooks and research books on a range of themes in systems thinking, from theoretical introductions to the systems thinking approach and its history, through practical guides to the implementation of systems thinking in the world, through to in-depth case studies that are significant for their profound impact.

This series is an essential reference point for anyone looking for innovative ways to effect systemic change or engaging with complex problems.

Managing Creativity
A Systems Thinking Journey
José-Rodrigo Córdoba-Pachón

Systems Thinking for a Turbulent World
A Search for New Perspectives
Anthony Hodgson

For more information about this series, please visit: www.routledge.com/ Systems-Thinking/book-series/STHINK

Systems Thinking for a Turbulent World

A Search for New Perspectives

Anthony Hodgson

Routledge
Taylor & Francis Group

LONDON AND NEW YORK

First published 2020
by Routledge
2 Park Square, Milton Park, Abingdon, Oxon OX14 4RN

and by Routledge
52 Vanderbilt Avenue, New York, NY 10017

Routledge is an imprint of the Taylor & Francis Group, an informa business

© 2020 Anthony Hodgson

The right of Anthony Hodgson to be identified as author of this work has been asserted by him in accordance with sections 77 and 78 of the Copyright, Designs and Patents Act 1988.

British Library Cataloguing-in-Publication Data
A catalogue record for this book is available from the British Library

Library of Congress Cataloging-in-Publication Data
Names: Hodgson, Anthony, author.
Title: Systems thinking for a turbulent world : a search for new perspectives / Anthony Hodgson.
Description: Abingdon, Oxon ; New York, NY : Routledge, 2020. | Series: Systems thinking | Includes bibliographical references and index.
Identifiers: LCCN 2019029187 (print) | LCCN 2019029188 (ebook) | ISBN 9781138594173 (hardback) | ISBN 9781138598676 (paperback) | ISBN 9780429486203 (ebook)
Subjects: LCSH: Decision making. | System theory. | Critical thinking. | Strategic management. | Organizational change.
Classification: LCC HD30.23 .H626 2020 (print) | LCC HD30.23 (ebook) | DDC 658.4/032—dc23
LC record available at https://lccn.loc.gov/2019029187
LC ebook record available at https://lccn.loc.gov/2019029188

ISBN: 978-1-138-59417-3 (hbk)
ISBN: 978-1-138-59867-6 (pbk)
ISBN: 978-0-429-48620-3 (ebk)

Typeset in Celeste and Optima
by Apex CoVantage, LLC

Contents

Figures

Tables

Acknowledgements

The viewpoint in this book is based on several decades of my own search for meaning in the fields of strategic thinking. Weaving the ideas together has the effect of taking them out of the time period in which I came across them and even worked on them in greater depth. However, I would like to express my appreciation for many of the people who have influenced and nourished the process in roughly chronological order.

In my twenties I was privileged to be appointed by J. G. Bennett as his senior research fellow at the then Institute for the Comparative Study of History, Philosophy and the Sciences. The conversation and projects with him and his small cohort of research fellows alerted me to the potential of qualitative systems thinking and the vast reach in time and space of Bennett's thinking, expressed in the four volumes of *The Dramatic Universe*. At that same time, a short period of study with David Bohm revolutionised my appreciation of alternative cosmologies and reinterpreting the nature of the universe. Influential colleagues at that time were Anthony Blake and Henri Bortoft. These foundations could not have happened without the sponsorship of Stafford Beer.

Applying some of these ideas to education led to the development of visual facilitation and cognitive kinetics, which would keep developing over decades of practice in management consulting. Rodney Myers was a crucial friend through this early period. The development of cognitive kinetics led to introducing hexagons for systems thinking to Shell Global as an aid to managing the complexity of strategic scenario planning. I am indebted to the deep interest in this work taken by Kees van der Heijden and later Arie de Geus, David Kreutzer and John Morecroft, through which I became convinced that strategic thinking needed to incorporate systems thinking and futures thinking. I was also privileged to work closely with Charles Hampden-Turner on the nature of dilemmas and the facilitation of their resolution.

This synthesis was greatly accelerated and intensified, forming a partnership with Gary Chicoine, who deepened a range of methods and helped give them practical form. The fundamentals of repatterning became clearer through this partnership. An invitation to introduce this work to Hewlett Packard Labs led me to work closely with Bill Sharpe and Ian Page, who saw the potential and disciplined me to codify more precisely how good concepts could become good shared thinking processes. It also led me to work closely with Ian Kendrick at Fujitsu to develop foresightful strategies in the then unknown territory of the emerging Internet and the nature of ethos-based communities. Bill and Ian have since 'retired' into becoming close research and development associates in the ideas in this book.

In parallel to this consulting work I met Graham Leicester and joined him as a founding member of the International Futures Forum (IFF) to address 'sustaining hope in a world we no longer understand and cannot control'. Fifteen years of close involvement and collaboration have greatly broadened and deepened the horizons of my work, especially that with Martin Albrow on social integrities and Max Boisot on the nature of knowledge. Graham with Maureen O'Hara clarified the three stages of conceptual, existential and actual emergency. Also in that group was Napier Collyns, who encouraged me to write. Graham's contribution to the understanding of the urgent role of transformative innovation is one of the keys to navigating in turbulent times.

I am grateful to the IFF for sponsoring the research that led to my PhD in systems science with Gerald Midgely and Angela Espinosa at the University of Hull, where I was able to go deeper into the issues of integrating systems thinking with futures thinking and the role of second-order science as an emerging paradigm enabling their integration. At that time, Roberto Poli of the University of Trento introduced me to the power of anticipation as a further enrichment of the synthesis. Timo Hämäläinen's interest in the second-order paradigm led to a rich transdisciplinary workshop that further cross-fertilised the ideas. Karl Muller enhanced my understanding of second-order cybernetics; Tom Flanagan, my appreciation of participation in dialogic design.

I am also grateful to Daniel Wahl for his interest in systems thinking in the field of global sustainability and his development of the regenerative culture theme emerging as a third-horizon vision and a second-horizon practice. Ioan Fazey brought in and tested these facilitation methods in research at the University of Dundee, which has also been enabled by a research fellowship in the School of Social Sciences. I am also grateful to Alfonso Montuori for introducing me to the work of Edgar Morin and his thinking about complexity.

The convergence of this work into a book is greatly inspired by my colleagues in the H3Uni team and their commitment to contributing to an education approach better suited to navigating the unknowns and uncertainties of the Anthropocene world we have brought upon ourselves.

Throughout the latter two decades of my consulting work, I was deeply inspired by my business partner and mentor, Gary Chicoine. His direct insight into the yoga of thinking propelled me into a deeper understanding in practice of the cognitive methods described in this book. He is a teacher par excellence of how to thrive in a world of high agency and high uncertainty through drawing on deeper sources in our self-nature.

I am indebted to my friend of many years, Don Tait, for his rendition of the ox herding icons based on Kaku-an from 12th century Japan.

My daughters, Rebecca and Ali, gave me their ears and comments to develop the story of my search in the book. My wife, Liz, has provided support, forbearance of my distraction and deep appreciation for this post-retirement project.

Preface

This book is about how we manage or attempt to manage the world and some of the deeply ingrained assumptions that dominate our thinking. Let me illustrate this with a traditional fable.

Once there was a wizard who lived in a remote castle on an island. His reputation spread far and wide throughout the land. Many sought him out to learn his secrets, but he would not allow them on the island. One young man was so persistent that he allowed him to stay to see if he was capable of being an apprentice. However, there were conditions for his stay. One of them was that he was only to watch the wizard about his work, not join in. Another was that he was to thoroughly clean the castle. The young man assumed that this would just be for a few weeks before he got to actually engage in the spell-making to cause amazing things to happen. But months, not weeks, went by, and he became increasingly frustrated whilst trying to appear content.

One unusual day the wizard announced that he would be away for a couple of days and that when he returned the hapless apprentice was to have thoroughly washed all the castle floors. He set to work with just the bucket and mop which was all the wizard had given him to carry out the task which also involved carrying water up many stairs from the well in the basement. It was tough work and soon the apprentice got tired, yet most of the castle floors still needed washing. He started thinking,

> I have seen the wizard do amazing things with his spells that he pulls out of one of his books of spells. He could easily have used magic to get the castle clean. Why don't I find a spell that would make the mop walk the stairs to the well and bring up a bucket of water every time it was needed?

So he looked through the enormous book and found such a spell. After several attempts and false starts, he finally activated the mop and to his delight it automatically brought water, mopped an area of floor and then repeated the process over and over. The apprentice settled down to look at more interesting and forbidden things and help himself to the wizard's food store.

Things were going well and much faster than he expected and by the end of the first day the job was done. He uttered the spell to stop the process and return the mop to its normal state. But to his growing horror, however, what he tried didn't work. The mop went on fetching water faster and faster and by the middle of the second day whole areas of the castle were filling up with water. It was a disaster. In desperation he took an axe and chopped the mop in two. He was greatly relieved that the activity stopped. He returned to his distractions.

This calm was interrupted by the sound of water being poured from *two* buckets. To his surprise and consternation both halves of the mop had resurrected and were fetching water twice as quickly. In desperation he wielded the axe again. The activity stopped for a short while and then renewed itself with double the vigour. The castle was now being thoroughly ruined by the deluge of water that poured all through it, with items floating around and debris piling up.

Two days had gone by, and despite the trouble he was in he desperately awaited the return of the wizard's superior spell to put a stop to it all. But the wizard didn't return. We are not sure if the apprentice drowned. There has been no news so far, and the island has sunk out of sight.

Those of you familiar with the traditional version of this story may wonder why in this version the wizard does not return and put things right. Let me explain. This little story is becoming a metaphor for the predicament of mankind.

Great Nature, the wizard of the evolution of the planet, the biosphere and us humans has worked her magic over billions of years. Only recently have we humans begun to unlock those secrets, especially by the invention of science and its application through technology. Broad revolutions have occurred – agricultural, industrial, materials extraction, communications, artificial intelligence, the Internet of things – which have enabled the colonisation of the planet and the spread of convenience, for example in the form of energy slave equivalents.

But this is being achieved at an approaching catastrophic cost. The impact of humanity on the planet is now considered to be of geological proportions and labelled the 'Anthropocene'. And the more we try to fix it, the faster it grows. The more we learn what needs doing to fix it, the more there is to do and less time to do it in. Humanity is the hapless apprentice of Great Nature who has over-reached and is jeopardising the whole situation. Great Nature is not interested in the minuscule time-frames of human generations and human awareness. We are on our own. *There is no wizard to come to the rescue* in our own time-frame.

Many shifts of mentality and attitude are needed to cope with and dampen down the turbulence that largely we, as a runaway species, have stirred up. This book addresses only one of them – the way we think about the nature of the world and hence how we believe we need to act in it. After over three hundred years of specialisation and 'divide and conquer', it is time to visit the neglected orientation of wholeness. The wholeness of which I speak is not some fuzzy, cosy state of mind but a rigorous shift in world-view, in the whole basis of what constitutes science and knowledge and what its relationships are to the actual world we live in. It is the condition needed to reverse our most threatening trends.

This is hard work. It has occupied me for over sixty years and still seems a daunting prospect. But there are some hopeful though largely disregarded signs. One is the emergence in the last fifty years of systems thinking as a discipline to reintegrate specialisation and take a more organic approach to knowing. Another is the development of futures thinking and foresight as something that can have method and be practiced rather than exist only in the domain of mythical oracles. A third is the growing recognition that the Newtonian/Cartesian legacy of mechanistic determinism, successful though it has been so far, has now become part of the problem and needs the presence of consciousness as an explicit aspect of effective knowledge.

In this book I gather some of these threads together as an offering to those who are seeking different ways of thinking about the further possibilities of systems thinking developing from second-order cybernetics and combining this with active foresight and the integration of both with the practice of facilitating collective intelligence. It is a progress report on an expedition which I hope others will take up since it is but a waystation on a longer journey for at least the next century.

The book is threaded together using the metaphor of a search for meaning taken from a Buddhist teaching of the 'stages of ox herding'. Each step in the search has its own quality of questioning and discovering. The journey of the original steps is towards enlightenment. In this work the steps lead to a new paradigm of systems thinking suited to turbulent times. With this structure you may consider three ways of reading the book. If you read just the preface and the ox-herding introduction to each chapter, you will get an overview of the theme of the book. If you read each chapter, you will find the main ideas that are the substance of the book and develop its thesis. If you use notes and the bibliography, you can build up a picture of the diverse sources of ideas that are woven together in the thesis.

Introduction

Our perspective determines what we can see. If what we are seeing is a fragmented and conflicted world, that is a function of our perspective. We might realise that we need a fresh viewpoint, but the catch is that we are not aware of our own perspective and so deny ourselves the possibility of significant change. Anything we may believe is fresh will be locked into our unconscious perspective. The philosopher Nagarjuna pointed out that the cause of all human suffering is that we take the relative to be absolute (Ramanan, 1966). Since in our world there are many relatives, each claiming to be absolute, it is no wonder that the world of human society is fragmented and in danger of destroying itself.

This book describes a personal learning journey with the aim of taking some of the absolutes and seeking to place them in a perspective of relationship. I call this 'open holism'. There are two aspects to this – a holistic approach challenges us to identify the unique nature and the specific value of every specific standpoint. Openness requires that we are not confined to any single point of view. Relative viewpoints, taken as absolute, will inevitably be contradictory and in conflict. The requirement to be true to what is intrinsic and useful in each of them denies any of them an absolute truth. Further, their proposed relationship in some more inclusive overview will inevitably contradict the logic of any one of them.

There is the risk that the integration of ideas, even if moderately successful, can fall into the trap of becoming another absolute. My approach is based on the view that any world-view is limited and applicable only to a limited domain of the vast, unexplored universe (Bohm & Hiley, 1993); therefore, the criteria for success are more about the extent to which such an integration transcends the fragmentation in a way that improves the way we interact and harmonise with the world. Does the integration reduce the negative effects on the fragmentation? Does the inclusive overview stimulate movement towards wholeness and healing?

For example, if we view our environment as inanimate, we will tend to treat it as being there for us to exploit for our benefit. If we view the world as a mutually interdependent living system, we are more likely to work with rather than against the environment.

The condition of being locked into a perspective unconsciously does not mean that we are not smart. Within a given perspective, great intelligence can be present. However, I will call that condition 'blind intelligence', borrowing a phrase from the systems philosopher Edgar Morin (Heath-Carpentier, in press). In this condition we will do clever things but in a way that jeopardises our situation whilst believing we are solving problems. Blind intelligence takes the understanding of a constrained domain and applies it to everything. From a wider perspective and a larger time-scale, a solution that works in a constrained domain applied more widely can be making things far worse. It can be storing up trouble for the future.

In this book, what is new is the way that the ideas have been configured and related to each other, bringing out certain implications for our human-planetary situation. I have brought this range of ideas to bear on systems thinking to gain a wider perspective. The book is largely about what I call pattern thinking and is itself the result of practising such pattern thinking.

The consequence of this is that ideas, well known within a limited specialist viewpoint, are brought together with others in a way that those specialties themselves are likely to contest or treat as taboo. For example, the presence of the subject is excluded from science in order to achieve 'objectivity'. In literature and anthropology the subject is central. The objective schools of thought reject the subjective as 'woo-woo', whereas the subjective schools of thought reject deterministic schools as inhuman.

My focus in this work is to question the assumptions or paradigms that mutually exclude each other and bring them into a larger viewpoint that can include their value but in a modified way and in mutual relation to each other. However, this is not a simple additive process, because, consistent with systems thinking, when separate things are connected, they modify each other and change each other's significance.

The power of specialisation in the discovery of new knowledge has been very successful, leading to an explosion of technology and its exploitation. However, this success has been in an unquestioned background of increasing fragmentation. As well as the multiplying divisions of knowledge, there is the increasing split between humans and their environment. In a single human being these would be regarded as indicators of ill health and an absence of wholeness. For the human-planet system, it is a breakdown of sustainable viability. Humanity is caught in a vicious cycle resulting from blind, fragmented intelligence. We are smart but in restricted ways that blind us to the causation of our current major challenges, including climate change, species extinction, unsustainable footprint and increasing social inequity and conflict. This now covers the whole planet and leaves us with nowhere else to go to escape the issue. We are becoming relatively used to the wider context of life being turbulent, but multiple exponential growths (Steffen, 2015) now create a context of hyperturbulence which we are decidedly not used to. The trends and our inability so far to change them indicate this as inevitable.

Chapter 1 addresses this challenge as a matter of healing this fragmented world and restoring a higher degree of health. One contribution to this process is focused on that of systems thinking. Why is this relevant? Despite its limitations, systems thinking is a vital though by no means complete contribution to resolving this challenge. Put simply, without joined up thinking, the patterns of relationship that need to be established to turn things around will simply not be recognised and developed; the necessary conversations will not take place. This is true for wholeness in medicine, education, business and even politics. It is especially true for the community of science, which, despite its protestations to be interested in new knowledge, ensures that it is kept within tightly prescribed limits.

Chapter 1 explains some of the distinctions that systems thinking makes from linear thinking, especially the way that effects can be causes and create dynamic loops which exhibit non-linear behaviour. This basic systems thinking is applied to the role and power of world-views over the human mind and how such viewpoints tend to reinforce themselves in a closed loop. The misjudgement of projecting linear thinking onto situations that are in fact systemic is illustrated. Systems thinking is also positioned as a phase in a spectrum from highly focused reductionism as an explanatory principle to the notion of a qualitatively infinite universe.

The first step of integration is to notice the way in which scientific materialism has had great success in those areas where exclusion of the observer works. Objectivity is held as a pillar of scientific wisdom, with the result that it is blind to the sentient nature of any observation. Chapter 2 proposes the rehabilitation of the observer as essential for a holistic world-view that is able to encompass the fact that people are subjects who constrain what can be understood by their expulsion from the object of study. The manner in which the researcher engages with research has profound implications for which modes of knowing are permitted and whether certain aspects, such as ethics and systemic consequences, are taken into account.

In the language of systems thinking, the acknowledgement of the observer leads to second-order cybernetics, in which the subject is always part of the system under investigation. Seven different aspects of second-order science are outlined with the proposition that some minimal admixture of these is necessary to apply systems science in a holistic way. I believe this is also a condition for strategic decision-making, which is described in Chapter 5. Especially important is the role of reflexivity, which requires the decision-maker to be self-aware of the kinds of assumptions that are determining perception, interpretation and judgement, not simply 'the facts'.

But before decision integrity can be understood, it is necessary to consider the implications of the time horizon of decisions. Further, I believe it is also necessary to re-examine our assumptions about the nature of time itself. This is investigated in Chapter 3. Cultural assumptions overlay our interpretation of time and are deeply conditioned into our attitudes toward life. Anthropologists have studied how time is understood in different cultures, and there is a greater richness of perception here than that which prevails in western societies, where the clock and the calendar rule (Gell, 1992; Novotny, 1994). To enrich our framing of time, I introduce in the chapter the idea of multiple time-like dimensions, of which the ticking of the clock is only one. Based on studies I made with John Bennett (1966), the framing extends from the four dimensions of space-time to seven dimensions. The purpose of this new framing is not to propose some grand theory of everything but to alert us to modes of perception which I believe are natural to us but blocked out by our culture. Stepping into this view can trigger a perception of the nature and accessibility of the future. This opens up more possibilities for change and transformation. Applying the three horizons concept is introduced as a method for reperceiving the future (Sharpe et al., 2016).

The next step is to consider whether these two steps of reframing, namely rehabilitating the observer and reperceiving the future, can increase our capacity to navigate hyperturbulence. This requires the modification of what has been described as systems thinking in Chapter 1. Despite the development of second-order thinking over the last sixty years, systems science is largely stuck in the first-order set of assumptions. The system is out there, and practitioners operate *on* the system. The view of systems is also based on the idea of feedback – that effects can be causes. Feedback is essentially performance information coming from the past. The time interval can be very small (as in-flight control computations of a supersonic fighter plane) but still structured around linear time. In Chapter 4, a development in biology of a model of the anticipatory system of life (Rosen, 1985) is brought into a second-order perspective. The new possibilities of this is that anticipatory systems are able to 'make use of the future' and that if they are second-order, they can access a wider spectrum of that future. Nevertheless, all this has to take place in the present moment, that is to say the total span of awareness of the decision-maker. Here lies a paradox. To consider these possibilities is a challenge to our dominant mind-set and obstacles are readily put up to looking at choice and responsibility this way. On the other hand, I believe that we humans have latent capacities to be more alert to seeing the future in the present. These perspectives are integrated into a new concept, the 'anticipatory present moment' (APM; Hodgson, 2018).

Information from the future is an increasingly interesting aspect of the recognition that, alongside matter and energy, information is an inherent property of the universe (Davies, 2019).

In the context of the APM we can now take a fresh look as to what decision integrity in the face of hyperturbulence looks like and how to improve it. In a world of hyperturbulence the rate of change and the dislocation caused by emergence of new patterns are such that we cannot have adequate information in the areas of human concern that matter. 'Big Data' and supercomputer power harnessed by artificial intelligence can learn and adjust to past turbulence but cannot deal with matters of values, ethics and conscience in the midst of a technologised society. It simply accelerates the process of machine displacing man.

Technologised decision-making assumes that a set of choices can be formulated. Of course many things can. But the serious challenges we have, whether personal or on the scale of the whole planet, are by their nature undecidable. Chapter 5 is addressed specifically as an approach to those important areas of life – provoked by hyperturbulence – in which our culture leads us to seek simplistic solutions to complex challenges. This step requires us to relax the hold of rationality as well as the hold of irrationality in our management of human affairs and seek instead new ways of navigating change and transformation that allow for enhanced ways of human knowing and deeper acknowledgement of intrinsic ethical responsibility beyond imposition of moral rules. In a world where the serious consequences of the situation are beyond the 'technological fix' and the political 'silver bullet', new ways of engaging with each other are needed in a way that treats decision as a learning process on several levels. In a world of no right answers and no experts, effective living is shifting from a set pattern to a journey of perpetual discovery.

This requires a radical change in the way we work and collaborate together. The dominant forms of meeting, organising, handling knowledge and sharing experience are too inefficient and too self-interested for success in a hyperturbulent environment. This is the focus of Chapter 6. The inefficiencies in the way we work together have several sources – some psychological, some physical and some cultural. For effective collaboration, a group of people need to be in a geometry, where each can see the others face to face, where the physical context – furniture, walls, visual tools – is congruent with equality of participation and where the culture is one of building on ideas through attentive listening. Creativity requires temporary suspension of judgement to let the ideas and interpersonal exchanges flow before applying judgement. A useful process guide is to travel through the stages of divergence, emergence and convergence.

Once those conditions are established, there need to be ways of more easily sharing pattern thinking. New tools are needed that take advantage of the gestalt psychology of pattern recognitions and meaning. Techniques are needed of pattern deconstruction and reconstruction. Processes and protocols that include everyone ('all voices will be heard') are needed. Repatterning or reperception needs a dynamic form of thinking rather than a fixed static 'holding to ideas'. This is an emotional and cultural challenge that requires, at least in the early stages, a particular kind of facilitation. It requires 'transformation in the now', the subject of Chapter 7.

The basic principle of transforming in the now or the present moment is that, for transformation, we need to find the resources right now (there is no tomorrow, for instance) in our experience. Facilitation of repatterning begins with the self-repatterning of the facilitator. This requires a kind of mindfulness which alerts us both to modes of perception and knowing that we take for granted and do not consciously use and to latent perceptions that we habitually tune out. These are the 'weak signals' that we refer to as hunches, intimations, precognitions and even dream-like visions. These usually present themselves as incongruent with our current pattern of perceptions or view of reality. Transformation requires reperception.

Four modes of anticipation are characterised that give these fleeting glimpses or wayward conceptions a place to be understood and noted. In this chapter, I prescribe examples of practices that help cultivate this greater alertness to the range of information we have available right now to make a difference. Indeed, information has been described as 'the differences that make a difference' (Bateson, 1972). These practices, shared by a collaborating group, increase the possibility of information from the future, which is the feedforward component of the APM mentioned in Chapter 4.

The various underlying components of a new developing practice are now in place. The proposition in Chapter 8 is that the synthesis of these components is already inherent in our make-up and that our problem in navigating through a hyperturbulent world is the prevailing cultures that diminish our awareness and alertness to our inherent capacity. In the spirit of open inquiry, there are two ideas that help us reframe our outworn cultural prejudices and experiment with some different approaches. One is the idea of systemic reality as a recurrent participative process in which we frequently reflect on the nature of our shared patterning, thus opening up the possibility to change it to better fit our circumstances (Sharpe, 2013). The other is the idea of dilemmas – which give us a way of readdressing the tensions and conflicts that hyperturbulence evokes – as opportunities for creative synthesis and innovation (Hampden-Turner, 1990).

These two ideas indicate an enrichment of systems thinking. One extends the notion of system to the notion of pattern not as a fixed structure but as a dynamic structuring that can appear stable through habitual participation or that can change through reflective awareness opening up ways to shift the pattern. The other opens up the space for systems thinking to acknowledge our human awareness as part of the system and facilitate an integration of the world of facts with the world of values.

The reader is invited to visit the opening systems diagram in Figure 1.1, which shows the way world-view has implications for action and its consequences. If this book does indeed outline some fresh configuration of the pattern of our world-view, there are potential consequences that will contribute to the positive loop and mitigate the negative loop. Actions emerging from systemic awareness as described will increase our capacity to anticipate, take decisions of greater integrity, increase our shared capacity for transformative innovation through creative collaboration and redesign our environment and technology to support these capabilities rather than extinguish them.

The stages of exploratory research

Running through the book is a spirit of inquiry stretching over several decades. This is very much an internal journey in relation to the questions and the content. As such, it is intrinsic to my own experience as much as it is to the ideas and information I have encountered. In terms of the ideas introduced in this book, especially in Chapter 2, this inquiry is a second-order system. I find it helpful to relate the sequence in this book to the metaphorical stages of personal search from the Zen tradition known as 'the stages of ox herding'. These depict the stages of seeking a seemingly elusive consciousness and self-understanding through a quest which has several distinct qualities. Each stage has a particular quality of mind in relating the inner to the outer, the awareness to that of which one is aware. Each chapter is linked to one of these stages to give a feel for the journey of inquiry independent from but related to the sequence of ideas.

In an early version there were eight stages, although the traditional version now has ten. I have taken the eight-stage version and consolidated the ninth and tenth into the eighth. Each chapter has an associated stage as an introduction resonating with my journey of inquiry. For those readers interested in the intuitive, this may be of especial interest. Otherwise, it is at least a road-map indicating the steps that each chapter makes. To help orientation here is a summary of the steps.

Step 1 – Seeking the ox
Things are not working and provoke a search for something better – enhancing systems thinking.

Step 2 – Finding the tracks
An approach is discovered – namely including the observer as legitimate.

Step 3 – First glimpse of the ox
A promising clue is found – understanding of the future needs to be reframed.

Step 4 – Catching the ox
Now, another view of system is possible – upframing the significance of anticipatory systems.

Step 5 – Taming the ox
The meaning of decision is changed – harmonisation of inner and outer through integrity.

Step 6 – Riding the ox home
The insights illuminate collective intelligence – the application of participative repatterning.

Step 7 – The ox out of sight, the self alone
The realisation of wholeness – all is now in the present moment of the system which includes us.

Step 8 – Entering the market place with helping hands
Self and source united – we can release the systemic capacities we need because they are latent.

However, congruent with systems thinking, this is not simply a linear process – it is a recurrent, interconnected pattern that is a journey of continuous learning as our turbulent world unfolds.

Chapter 1

Healing our fragmented world

Step 1 – Seeking the ox

Are we missing something? We have a hunch it is the 'ox'. The ox is strangely familiar yet not in sight.

Here lies the challenge. How do we seek for something which we know needs to be different from what we have tried so far and which we don't know how to recognise? It is going to require new insights that we are likely to find only by looking in unfamiliar places with unfamiliar mental orientations. Insight is a characteristic of persons; there is a 'who' that is engaging the insight. What marks a real insight is that whoever has it cannot turn back – the genie is out of the bottle. Yet there is a peculiar quality in insights of discovery which can be summed up as the quality 'not yet'. We get a glimmer of something different – a different pattern – yet much work remains to be done to reveal it. There are many stages between a hunch and a realisation.

Following on from the sorcerer's apprentice story, how are we to rescue ourselves from our predicament if there is no source of wisdom with the insight and power needed to slow and then reverse the harmful trends whilst setting up a more resilient society capable of thriving in what are most likely to be dramatically changed planetary conditions? The answer must surely lie in a growing sense of mutual responsibility amongst peoples, irrespective of their origins, backgrounds, allegiances and personal belief systems. But supposing the increasing shocks from the distressed global system do alert a sufficient number of people of goodwill – will our current knowledge base be adequate for the task? There are those who claim that we have all the needed solutions but are incapable of implementing them. My belief is that this very claim is blind to the fact that we are embedded in a whole system in which the separation of technology from humanity, of humanity from planetary well-being and the assumption that the earth is simply there for heedless exploitation is one of the main drivers of the crisis. We need to seek for something radically different in both our worldview and our practical knowledge. In the stages of spiritual ox herding, for us, the ox represents the new way of thinking we need.

To look for a better future we need to be able to step out of our comfort zone in the small daily present and explore a much wider and deeper present moment.

This is the first stage of ox herding.

~~~~~

Thinking differently

Why do we need a different way of thinking about the world from our usual way of regarding it? And why is the development of systems thinking (Ramage & Shipp, 2009) a promising step towards that different way of thinking? This book sets out to answer those questions with some new thinking about systems, their nature and their relevance to practical affairs in the turbulent complexity and uncertainty that increasingly pervades the world.

The scale and disruption caused by the life of eight billion humans on the planet is now considered to be on a geological scale. What this means is that the combined impact of all our activities is actually changing the surface of the planet – lithosphere, biosphere and atmosphere. We have released tens of thousands of chemicals and substances not previously in the environment. These have known and unknown effects on all life – for example, false oestrogens, carcinogenic compounds and islands of plastic floating in the oceans. We are witnessing a mass extinction of life comparable to the impact of the massive asteroid that wiped out the dinosaurs.

There is always a background rate of extinction, but presently it is esti-mated to be up to ten thousand times that background rate. Sufficient green-house gases have been released such that they are almost certain to raise the global temperature (especially that of the oceans) beyond thresholds that permanently disrupt ecosystem habitats (e.g. coral reefs as indicators). Beyond these material and biological conditions there are massive social, cultural and political disruptions. In a global economy where ownership of materials, land and processes is in the hands of very few whilst a sixth of humanity does not even have potable water and secure habitats, there are massive pent-up tensions and inequalities.

The vicious cycle of multiple escalating conditions of the Anthropocene[1] is driving attempts to cope with the changes, but these responses are unco-ordinated. Fragmented fixes further exacerbate the problems with multi-ples fixes that fail. With almost eight billion humans driving this escalation, we have no collective capacity for wisely coordinated initiatives that will both alleviate urgent issues and simultaneously safeguard long-term vision of sustainability. Behind this fragmentation lies a source problem – frag-mented minds do not have the needed capacity for wholeness. To navigate this turbulent world we need a healing – an integration of our minds to greater wholeness.

For this to be possible we need to appreciate the nature of turbulence in this environment of change and complexity. Our highly technologised and compartmentalised society depends on the persistence of flow. The eco-nomics of distribution, for example, have led to a 'just in time' logistics upon which we depend for food and goods. We may think that this flow is sustained by clever systems we have designed. But they are clever only in a relatively stable environment where we understand what is going on.

But suppose that the environment is changing and that conditions are emerging that increasingly depart from our understanding. When flow is disturbed, it changes into turbulence and disrupts our expectations about what will happen and what we can depend on. Water may flow smoothly down a stream bed until it hits a rock; then, turbulence radically changes the pattern of the flow. Navigating turbulence can be compared to canoeing white water rapids when a new level of skill is required, and even entirely new skills like the Eskimo roll that allows recovery from capsize when the going gets too rough.

This new level of skill can be called adaptive capacity, which determines the capability of a system to receive feedback from its environment and respond quickly enough to get back on course. For this to happen, the system has to have affordances build in that enable this. There is no time for constructing them in the heat of the moment. For example, the closed nature of a kayak permits the Eskimo roll but this is not possible in an open Canadian style canoe.

Adaptive capacity may turn out to be accidental or peripheral in a system. It is likely to be limited in its range of response. Knowing there is 'white water ahead' might enable new capacities to be developed deliberately ahead of when they need to be applied. This already requires the adaptive requirement of anticipation, structural modification and new skill development. This can be seen in the development of effective emergency services where full-scale rehearsal of disasters enable practice and learning ready for the real thing should it happen.

Turbulence can now be seen as a condition where the changes in the environment exceed the adaptive capacity of the society. If that gap is persistently widening, we can define a condition of hyperturbulence, also called a vortical environment.[2] To understand this we need to look at what happens to society as the gap opens up. There is a specific dynamic process. The social 'organism' begins to bifurcate. Sectors with higher adaptive capacity start to concentrate and draw a boundary with the rest, who are progressively excluded. There are many conditions that exhibit this ranging, from 'downsizing' to outright war.

Under these conditions the society may survive as a whole on the fringes of the concentration of adaptability. At least this is the case on smaller scales. But the conditions of the Anthropocene are global, and the maintenance of this defence against turbulence rapidly decreases in effectiveness and increases in expense. The nature of global changes, such as global warming and ocean degradation, populations growth and resource scarcity, are unavoidable. At best they can be postponed – although at an increasing cost. Apparently highly adaptive enclaves eventually become fortresses that cannot withstand the scale of the turbulence.

So the process begins with partition, which in turn erodes collaboration and increases isolation. The gap between 'haves' and 'have nots' widens. The adaptive sectors appropriate more and more resources, largely at the expense of the rest. The gap between short-term and long-term viability widens. Success to the successful today increases the conditions leading to a large crash of the whole system later. The adaptive capacity becomes locked into the short term and blind to the longer-term consequences.

Thus the global society becomes increasingly fragmented, and its assumptions lead to the creation of 'remedies' that actually exacerbate the problem. A fresh look at adaptive capacity is required, but the systemic nature of this change of viewpoint must first be taken into account. It is more than simply a change of mind or a change of policy. It is a fundamental problem of world-view.

Although each of us has a degree of uniqueness in our world-view, an important cultural factor is that we share certain beliefs and assumptions. Most of these are unexamined and lie outside our normal awareness. They condition us to believe that what we see and understand is reality. However, where there is a mismatch between that 'internal reality' and the external world, it generates problems. The pattern we have of personal values, beliefs, attitudes, assumptions and ideas has an impact on the world as well as on our response to the world-views of others. To the extent that we are unaware of these in ourselves, we are poorer as we navigate through life, especially in a turbulent environment. When this is compounded into a whole society, major discontinuities can occur as reality catches up with false assumptions.

Our current knowledge and understanding is clearly effective and relevant in many ways, but it is incomplete and in many cases no longer matches the circumstances we are immersed in. This would not be a problem if we were open to learning at a deeper level. However, our identity, as individuals or social groups, is so wrapped up in our fixed world-views that we have difficulty with learning that challenges our belief systems. The result of the absence of this level of learning is increasing mismatch and conflict.

On the other hand, if we can cultivate open learning, we have the possibility of transforming our understanding to new levels with increased congruence and effectiveness in relation to how the world is behaving. The faster that learning cycle, the better we will be able to navigate in a turbulence which requires a rapid and relentless shift in our world-view. It also opens us up to multiple ways of knowing. For example, if events are moving faster than our capacity for data gathering and analysis, our logical mode of knowing cannot keep up with the shifting landscape. If we are able to tap into other capacities which neuroscientists are highlighting, such as gut intelligence and heart intelligence, we may find ways of acting and reacting that are effective and that we otherwise we would not have arrived at.

Given that different cultures have different dominant world-views, reflecting different priorities the flexibility of learning also helps us to deal with world-views different from our own. We may be able to avoid unnecessary tensions and even learn from the differences. Multi-cultural learning is as important as transdisciplinary learning.

Figure 1.1 shows how our world-view system determines our interaction with the world and its consequences. How we see the world influences largely how we act. How we act impacts and provokes reaction from the world. Since the world is complex, there are usually factors at work that mean a simple linear cause-effect is not the way this works. In systems thinking this is called a 'causal loop', where effects become causes that reinforce the behaviours of the whole system. A familiar example is accumulating interest on a debt, where the next cycle of interest is calculated on the total of principal and previous interest. The result is an exponential growth of debt. How the world reacts determines the state

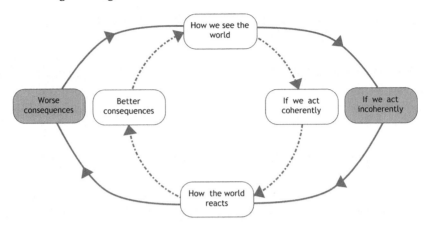

Figure 1.1 The positive and negative systemic consequences of world-view

of the world. The consequences may be a better situation or a worse situation depending on our analogy of whether we pay off the debt or not. Now comes the catch. We tend to interpret the consequences through the same mental model or belief system that we had at the beginning of the cycle. The belief system acts as a cognitive filter and tunes in what we want to believe and tunes out what we don't want to believe. It is as if the more we get into debt the more we spend. This is referred to in cognitive science as 'confirmation bias'. That means that the arrow linking consequences to how we see the world is reinforcing the problem as failure to learn; it is essentially a state of denial. Absence of learning causes increasing rigidity in the world-view. Even assuming benign motivation, this leads to a world of unintended consequences and repeating the same mistakes.

However, if the reaction to the world is open and learning, better consequences will result and the world-view is open to revision and improvement.

From this simple but profound system model we can now look more closely at the major mismatch arising from our current world-views. This mismatch is between a belief in linear change coming up against a massively accelerating change in the world. To explain this further we need to appreciate more deeply that the exponential curves of the Anthropocene are simply one snapshot of a process that is being driven by a deeper dynamic structure. That structure is systemic in the sense that the underlying invisible structures are systems with properties that do not follow our usual anticipations. Since structure is dynamic, it is also subject to being changed by the processes it configures. Stability is a temporary affair relevant to the overall time span of the process. It is different between organisms and mountains.

This condition has been elegantly summed up by Edgar Morin:[3]

> An intelligence that is fragmented, compartmentalized, mechanistic, disjunctive, reductionistic, breaks up the complexity of the world into disconnected fragments, splits up problems, separates what is connected, unidimensionalizes what is multidimensional. It is an intelligence that is at once short- and far-sighted, colorblind, and monocular. It ends up more often than not by being blind. It precludes the possibility of understanding and reflection, as well as any corrective judgement or long-term perspective. The more problems become multidimensional, the more there is an incapacity to conceive their multidimensionality. The more problems become planetary, the more they remain unthought. The more the crisis progresses, the greater our incapacity to conceive of the crisis. Incapable of envisioning the planetary context and complexity, blind intelligence makes us unconscious and irresponsible. It believes in the pertinence and the trustworthiness of its planning activities which often ignore the conditions, the constraints and possibilities, of the context for action.
>
> Consequently, as with natural catastrophes, there are human catastrophes with innumerable victims and consequences that cannot be accounted for let alone predicted.

Fragmentation renders anticipation difficult. A good deal of our anticipations are based on assumptions about causality. The most dominant one is that events or forces coming from the past cause the things which are happening in the present, and these, in turn, will determine what will happen in the future. This can be summarised as the 'linear assumption'. Sometimes it is conscious in the sense that we may use analytical trend analysis and make extrapolations. Mostly it is an unconscious taken-for-granted view of the way the world works. This has the effect of excluding another view, which is that behaviour over time is also determined by underlying structure. This is evident in the animal world where, for instance, the same context applied to a dog and a cat will lead to different behavioural outcomes. The differences between the make-up of the dog and that of the cat have a strong effect on what the response will be. We'll sum this up with a simple principle: *structure drives behaviour.*

As explained in the previous section on the role of world-view, this distinction between the linear and structural orientation leads to many of the difficulties of navigating turbulence. When we impose linear assumptions on a situation where structure drives behaviour, we end up with unintended consequences and perverse behaviours. Let's look at some illustrative examples.

There is a classic story of a king who had problems in his kingdom and sought help. The help came from a strange advisor who appeared at court.

The adviser claimed he could solve the problem but would expect payment. The king was so desperate that he said, 'Whatever you want!' The adviser noticed the king liked to play chess. He said he was very modest in his requirement and simply asked for one grain of rice on the first square of the chess board and for this to be doubled on every subsequent square. The king saw this as a bargain and agreed. However, when the adviser had succeeded and came to collect his due, the court treasurer informed the king that, by the time they reached the sixty-fourth square, this would be greater than all the rice stock in the entire kingdom.[4]

Ray Kurtzweil, the entrepreneur and inventor, used this metaphor to define the second half of the chessboard: an exponential growing factor commences a significant effect on the economic performance. The second half of the chessboard has over four billion times the rice grains as the first half! The implication in a turbulent environment is 'beware small perturbations'. If they are being driven by a new but hidden coupling, they could be the start of an exponential system which, if treated in a linear fashion, will provoke shocks and surprises.

Another example is the story of the lily pond. A gambler took a naïve person to see a lily pond early in the season. He pointed out that the small area covered by lilies tended to double every day. The pond was very big. He bet the other he could not calculate how long it would take to cover the entire pond at the point when the pond had become half-covered. Calculating growth rates, the other guy reckoned just a few days. He was astonished and lost his bet when it turned out to be only one day.

These two examples may seem trivial at first, but they illustrate an important principle about the disjunction between holding a world-view upon which we act and the behaviour of an actual world more complex than our mental models. This is especially the case when the disjunction has escalated to the scale of the entire planet. To explain this we need to look at some examples more complex than the gap between linear assumptions and exponential growth. These are runaway state, overshoot and collapse, and structural degradation.

A systems world-view

Supposing people's interpretations of the forecasts of global warming are based on linear assumptions which fail to take into account that the underlying structure could change and trigger an extreme non-linear effect. It would be like assuming the effects on a shoreline would be tidal when, in fact, a tsunami is triggered. The hypothesis of runaway climate change is one such example. Two important factors could change the whole dynamics of global warming – one is the evaporation of the oceans, increasing the blanket effect of water vapour; the other is the release of methane from the methane clathrates which are currently sequestering vast quantities of methane, a far more potent greenhouse gas than carbon dioxide. Both water vapour and methane are greenhouse gases much more effective than carbon dioxide. In the case of ocean warming, the increase in release of water vapour would feedback to increase the greenhouse effect and speed up warming. This could operate analogous to the rice and the lilies in an exponential growth that seems trivial at first but then steeply bends as it reaches the 'second half of the chessboard'.

The conditions for the escape of methane from permafrost add another factor that brings out the relevance of structure driving behaviour. The methane is trapped in the tundra or the ocean in a compound that, at a certain temperature, breaks down and releases the methane. The general warming induced by carbon dioxide may reach a threshold where the breakdown and release occur. Then, a gas twenty times the blanketing effect would be released and exponentially reinforce warming at a rate far greater than the original. This is the runaway effect. It is awakening the Kraken of climate change. This is an illustration of how the underlying structure that appears stable is subject to discontinuous change leading to totally different behaviour.

Overshoot and collapse is another threshold effect. Suppose we are growing a set of conditions in society that require resources, such as food. We have a way of doing that which has not yet reached its capacity. So the growth continues unabated and success is in the air. Then, at a certain point, a gap opens up where need outstrips supply. Coupled with this the supply starts breaking down from the demands made which disrupt the method of supply. This might have been dealt with if it had been picked up early enough and remedial action taken, but this perception was not in the linear world-view. Momentum is generated, and there is overshoot of demand over supply. Then the supply structure rumbles, and there is collapse of the whole system. This pattern has been noticed in organisations, industries, societies and even civilisations but almost invariably with hindsight, not with foresight. The systemic mental models were not present in the world-views of those in power to get the point. Or their vested interests in the old success wave were too compulsive to be sacrificed for a non-collapsing future.

Structural degradation occurs when the underlying structure upon which the function of a system depends, breaks down and that behaviour is no longer possible. A biological example would be the effect of ocean warming on coral reefs. As oceans warm they change the chemistry such that coral starts to die off and appear bleached; since coral is the substrate of a habitat and a complex ecology, this changes the whole system, which eventually collapses with most species of fish and plant dying off. A live sea becomes a dead sea. Subsequent cooling of the ocean does not restore the ecology because a structural change has taken place. The 'pattern that connects', as Bateson would put it, is fractured.

The patterns of behaviour shown in these examples illustrate a deeper principle behind structure determining behaviour which is called 'isomorphism'. 'Morph' means 'form' and 'iso' means the same, so isomorphism means 'of the same form'. So these kinds of disruptive behaviours may also occur in social systems where they are exacerbated by the projection of linear assumptions into a non-linear world. Underlying structure driving behaviour in similar patterns occurs at many levels. In systems science this is called recursion.

Many underlying structures are systemic nature and this gives them certain properties. First, the inner structure of a system contains variables that are strongly connected. This is part of the pattern that connects. The connections are dynamic such that changes in one variable will affect other variables either directly or indirectly depending on the linkages. Some of these linkages connect back to a variable earlier in the sequence. This forms a feedback loop where, for example, a variable A can effect a change in variable B. A linkage back from B into A causes a further change such that the effect has also become a cause. This is called a causal loop.

When the number of variables are large, the connections increase at a geometric rate and we have a complex system or more accurately a complex multi-system. In complex multi-systems a new layer of behaviour emerges called emergent properties. An emergent property is a new behaviour that could not be predicted from knowledge of the interacting components of the system. Even from a systems perspective it is a surprise!

Systems also can have a property that they are able to regenerate themselves, a property called autopoiesis or 'self-production'. Once a system with strong internal coupling exists it is difficult to change. We may prod it but it 'pushes back' to retain the coherence it has established. Indeed it is this coherence which enables us to recognise it as a system.

A system is also distinguished from its environment by a boundary. In living organisms this can be a cell wall or a skin. In social systems it may be more ephemeral, such as a behavioural convention. But to exist the systems have to have a minimum conformance or fit to its environment. It may also have a strong interdependency. The system-environment has a property called structural coupling. The state of this property will determine the fitting of the system into its environment. Maturana and Varela (1987) point out that *structural coupling occurs whenever there is a history of recurrent interactions leading to the structural congruence between two (or more) systems.*

The assumptions of linearity are deeply ingrained in the way we like to organise and habituate our relationship to the environment. Common devices like the accelerator pedal of a car are based on the principle of 'the more you press, the faster you go'. Most financial investments are based on the assumption of 'put more in to get more out'. However, as the impact of humans has reached geological proportions, it reveals existing and creates further complexities that in turn have emergent systemic properties, that generate behaviour we little understand and cannot anticipate.

To improve our anticipation we need more perceptive ways of thinking about the future and making decisions based on what we are learning from such exercises. Modelling tries to do this, but this is a slow and unreliable methodology since the methods of modelling tend to be increasingly complicated and fall into the trap of assuming that the complicated can model the complex. As a number of researchers have pointed out, these are two quite different domains.[5]

David Wasdell, in discussing runaway climate change,[6] makes this contrast with his story of the jaguar. The gist of the story is that a team of experts modelled all aspects of the jaguar's anatomy and physiology to work out what its maximum speed was, and this turned out to be just over 40 miles per hour. However, empirical studies filming jaguars on the run discovered their maximum speed was closer to 70 miles per hour. That difference in levels of speed has considerable survival and evolutionary implications. Models can help but they are always incomplete.

However, systems science and complexity science largely suffer from a limitation that the observer is excluded from the systems, which is treated as an 'objective' entity separated from the observer. By this exclusion in deterministic science we have made considerable progress but the new global situation is also showing up the weaknesses of this approach. There are unintended consequences. There are emerging disciplines that can help us take steps beyond this limitation – second-order cybernetics, observer participation, transdisciplinary connectedness and the state of the observer. They rarely get brought into the discussions. Overcoming this limitation can be rectified by considering more deeply the nature of complex thought advocated by Edgar Morin.[7] Gerald Midgley points out that any observation is in some sense an intervention, so even reductionism implies a position of interference in the nature of the object under investigation. This fact gets buried and then the fact that it has been buried itself gets buried. It becomes undiscussable or trivialised in mainstream society. Morin show that reductionism fragments and therefore evades the full challenge of complexity; even holism can easily become an abstraction which also does not address the essential requirement of including the observer in the observation.

> In either case, reductionist or holistic explanation seeks to simplify the problem of complex unity. The one reduces the explanation of the whole to the properties of the parts conceived in isolation. The other reduces the properties of the parts to the properties of the whole, also conceived in isolation. These two mutually repelling explanations each arose out of the same paradigm.[8]

The notion of complex thought embraces and interweaves both aspects of part and whole. It is a more insightful context for considering the relationship between the elements of time, pattern and perception through a reflexive view. The reflexive view affirms that the state of the human as a thinker is critical to the effectiveness of the human as a doer. There is a principle of correspondence – that we need complex thinking for a complex world and that we have gone past the point where simplification and specialisation alone are capable of dealing with the major issues we face. Simplification and specialisation without a complimentary layer of complex thought will surely drive the dynamic of unintended consequences rapidly up an exponential curve. A rethink about the nature and role of thinking[9] is required.

I find it useful to picture five layers of 'thinking into complexity', by which I mean how to engage my mind in different aspects of considering complexity which, if muddled, muddle the thinking. I distinguish these as linear analysis, systems concepts, complexity, reflexive systems and complex thought; all in some way reference a view of the underlying *pattern* of things and processes. Each of these five ways of thinking plays a role not only in the theoretical world but also in the practical world. Each of them has an associated set of application tools and procedures.

These are portrayed in Figure 1.2 as concentric circles, implying that the mental picture of complexity is shifting its nature, and its logic in moving

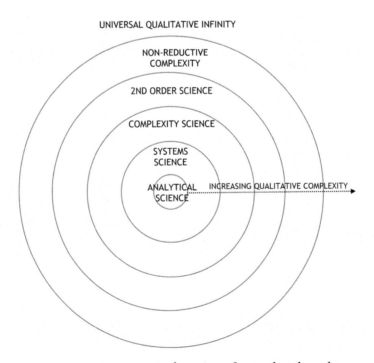

Figure 1.2 Concentric domains of complex thought

from one circle to the next. Also, the outer circles are not in contradiction with the inner but in some way contain them as an aspect. Each of them is an extensive field, so the description that follows is to indicate the general notion with the purpose of showing that systems thinking itself in my mind is only one layer of the complex, though it is needed for the hyperturbulent world.

Analytical science – the small explains the large by addition
This view describes the functioning of the whole by analysis of the parts on whatever scale is being considered.

Systems science – non-linear dynamic patterns
This is a view that causation can be circular as well as linear and that the non-linear behaviour requires a different kind of modelling and analysis.

Complexity science – emergent properties
This a view that complex situations as distinct from complicated ones are inherently unpredictable in certain respects through the phenomena of emergent properties.

Reflexive synthesis – reality as a two-way street
This is a view that how we see an understand the world has consequences for the world we are viewing.

Non-reductive complexity – the distinctiveness of authentic wholeness
This is a view that the holistic view is primary and the way we make distinctions and boundaries in thought or in practice is unavoidably reductive in some measure.

Qualitative infinity – the essential unfathomability of the universe
This is a philosophical and cosmological perspective which essentially proposes that any knowledge we have is unavoidably incomplete and claims for its absolute nature are misplaced.

The important thig is that they all are valid and all are subject to misplaced application. This book is concentrating on the second-order science.

A key reason for this state of affairs is that the processes of thinking that dominate our human affairs are incongruent with what is going on and what is actually needed. When the analytical science claims to be the sole arbiter of reality, the thought processes are no longer adequate to deal with the rising complexity. What is needed are new ways of thinking that are suited to navigating complexity and exploring the unknown and, above all, able to treat re-patterning as a norm rather than an exception. This distinction is between *static* thinking and *dynamic* thinking. To understand dynamic thinking we need to be able to step outside the boundaries we have established over recent centuries through privileging rationality as the most valid way of knowing. The new field of complex thought,[10] with its associated new methods and skills, needs to be established such that we become equipped to take on the challenges of the contemporary world as a positive, creative transformative change. Included in the new skills is the capacity to be humanly present in our thinking and actions, fully acknowledging the first person. This is the theme of the next chapter.

Notes

1 Olsson, P., Moore, M.-L., Westley, F. R., & McCarthy, D. D. P. (2017). The concept of the anthropocene as a game-changer: A new context for social innovation and transformations to sustainability. *Ecology and Society, 22*(2), 31.

2 Babüroğlu, O. N. (1997). The vortical environment: The fifth in the emery-trust levels of organizational environments, edited by E. L. Trist et al. *Tavistock Anthology, 3.* McCann, J. E., & Selsky, J. (1984). Hyperturbulence and emergence of type 5 environments. *The Academy of Management Review, 9*(3), 460–470.

3 Morin, E. (In press). *Confronting complexity.* A. Heath-Carpentier (Ed.). Albany: SUNY Press. p. 20.

4 The number is 18,446,744,073,709,551,615.

5 Snowden, D. J., & Boone, M. E. (2007). A leader's framework for decision making. *Harvard Business Review,* (November), 1–9.

6 Wasdell, D. *Climate dynamics: Facing the harsh realities of now.* Apollo-Gaia project, 5 October 2015. Retrieved from www.apollo-gaia.org/Harsh%20Realities.pdf
    'The value of Climate Sensitivity, on which this presentation is based, was derived from historical conditions in which change was slow, close to equilibrium and in response to which natural systems had time to adapt. Those conditions no longer apply. Anthropogenic change is at least 100 times faster than at any time in the Paleo record. The system has been driven far from equilibrium and smooth natural adaptation is no longer possible. In this situation many factors combine to drive a higher and increasing value for Climate Sensitivity'. p. vi.

7 'The concept of system requires the full employment of the personal qualities of the subject in its communication with the object. It differs radically from the classical concept of the object, which referred uniquely either to the "real" or to the ideal. Systems are profoundly related to the real. They are more real because they are more rooted in and linked with physis than the old quasi-artificial object and its pseudo-realism. At the same time, they are profoundly related to the human mind, that is to say, to the subject, which is itself immersed in culture, society, and history. The concept of system demands a natural science that is at the same time a human science' (Morin, 2008, p. 107).

8 Morin, E. (2008). *On complexity.* Cresskill, NJ: Hamilton Press. p. 101.

9 Geersten, H. R. (2012). Rethinking thinking about higher-level thinking. *Teaching Sociology, 31*(1), 1–19.

10 Morin, *On complexity.*

Chapter 2

Rehabilitating the observer

Step 2 – Finding the tracks

> *The insight dawns that all current interpretations are transient.*
> *Something more reliable is sought and clues come into sight.*

To find the clues for the missing ox, we need to question much more deeply a number of presuppositions. We are all actors on the stage of the earth, but we have fallen into a split between the knowledge and the knower. The knower is not supposed to be known but rather expunged to leave us with 'objective knowledge'. This enormously constrains the range of our perception so important features of the world and of ourselves that need to be taken into account are not even recognised. However, if we step back, reflect and question where we are coming from, we find that there is much in our world that we have not entertained. We have hung signs on them saying 'speculative', 'unverifiable', 'not susceptible to measuring and weighing', 'doesn't fit our world-view therefore cannot be true'. As a society of scientists we have given almost absolute official precedence to the quantitative and dismissed the qualitative as unscientific.

Yet science itself progresses by the entertaining of hypotheses, by speculating that something seemingly impossible might just be possible, that there can be multiple interpretations of the same phenomenon. If we do not speculate what *might be* that is different from the current received wisdom, we are blinded to seeing where there are actually clues that *it is*. So the seeker of new knowledge is not just an 'objective measuring device' but also potentially a sensitive and creative instrument in the world of the senses, the world of ideas and the world of meaning.

Most notable here is that the thing we are missing is not the world but ourselves. Any observation is made by an observer. Any piece of knowledge is known by someone. Any action in and on the world is made by people. Objectivity is an extreme case of subjectivity where we have agreed to eliminate ourselves from consideration without actually doing so. The clue lies in ourselves, the nature of our mind, our perception and thus how we engage with the world. This clue leads us towards a change of paradigm.

This is the second stage of ox herding.

~~~~~

Paradigm shift

The meaning of the term paradigm I am using here is taken from Edgar Morin's definition in his review of education for UNESCO:[1] Paradigm as 'The promotion/selection of master concepts of intelligibility'. The dominant paradigm of science determining its mode of intelligibility, including many aspects of systems science, leads to the manipulation of the 'out there' in ways that do not reference the wider systems, quantitative and qualitative, man-made and natural, that a given technology impacts upon. In so far as this has degrading effects on human beings, there are also implications for communities of scientists. Even if they protest otherwise, scientists are members of the human species! No piece of knowledge is actually value free. It is coloured by the assumptions of the knowledge producer.

I believe we are at a point where the nature of the science itself, its dominant paradigm, is unsuited in its present form to understand the nature of our global challenges and what is needed effectively to respond to them. A new paradigm is needed in our search for truth that goes beyond current science. This new paradigm will include the current science but only for those domains for which it is suited.

This problem is increasingly being investigated and is raising questions about the suitability of our historically inherited ways of knowledge production[2] and the kind of new transformational knowledge that is required to generate solutions in society to the problems, such as climate change, that have been identified. New essentials are being proposed[3] by Fazey and co-researchers that begin to shift the ground of science. For example,

1   Focusing on transformations to quite new operational patterns of how a society functions in a sustainable way;
2   Focusing on solution processes that place new knowledge in a context for action rather than just 'knowing about';
3   Valuing with equivalent status 'how to' practical knowledge alongside the 'knowing what' rather than as something added after the fact;
4   Placing research as occurring from within the system being investigated rather than as a disconnected observer assuming a *deus ex machina* position;
5   Acknowledging throughout the ethical responsibilities and consequential aspects of new knowledge rather than 'throwing this over the wall' to politicians and society to figure the implications out after the fact;
6   Seeking to transcend current thinking, which essentially means being open to the emergence of new patterns of thought that are better suited to the new complexities;
7   Taking a multi-faceted transdisciplinary approach to understand and shape change so that systemic effects are anticipated;
8   Acknowledging a range of roles that researchers can adopt that go beyond narrow academic and professional limitations;
9   Encouraging components of second-order science where the observer is acknowledged to be built in from the start on research programmes;
10 Incorporating reflective practice in researchers and their collaborators in relation to the whole process of transposing new knowledge into useful and appropriate application.

This set of recommendations reveals several breaks away from traditional science to provoke enriched systems of knowledge production directly relevant to the world of hyperturbulence.

As long as the paradigm of first-order science is so dominant, especially with the control of research funding and tertiary institutions, the chances of these considerations being taken up on any scale are weak. What is missing still is a larger consensus on the nature of second-order science, how it can be consciously incorporated into scientific practice and how it is understood to yield practical insights and results that are not accessible to first-order science, especially in the domain of navigating large-scale social and planetary uncertainty. This presents us with a paradox, namely that to enable a change of scale, speed and effectiveness in responding to complex challenges we need to pay much more attention to the personal dimension of how we, individually and collectively, can generate this kind of know-how. How the scientist and practitioners are personally present in their work and their communications becomes a crucial factor of the new level of effectiveness. This is more than having, say, skills of writing and presentation. It requires reflective practice and greater self-awareness and awareness of the deeper assumptions being made in scientific work. And this applies equally to systems science, with which we are concerned in this book.

In the search for truth beyond imaginative and unverifiable speculation science developed what it calls 'objectivity'. Certain rules came to determine the scientific endeavour. To remove speculative but unverifiable claims the scientist as observer was divorced from the observation. The observation, as empirical science, was valid only if it could be reproduced and tested by a wider community of scientists. The role of the scientist as person was placed in the background and subject increasingly to measurements that could also be reproduced. If theories were forthcoming, they had to point to experiments that could be carried out by dispassionate others who could reproduce the phenomena in question and discover the same parameters and measures.

The success of this approach over the last three hundred years of the expansion of science and technology is clear, especially its expansion over recent decades with such developments, for example, as orbital telescopes, decoding the genome and the capacity to create 'designer' molecules. Through these the universe is seen in greater extent and finer detail, the foundations of life being codified at the cellular level and the world of chemical molecules becoming visualisable at the atomic level.

This same science applied to the earth's condition has also revealed the parameters of planetary stability and its disturbance with such measures as the concept of 'safe operating space'[4] and the growing transgression of critical boundaries, of which global warming has become the most generally acknowledged.

However, this same science applied to the question of humanity's adaptive capacity is proving inadequate and too incongruent to deal with the complexity of the socio-political-ecological-technological challenge. For example, despite all efforts global temperature is still rising in the wake of continuously rising greenhouse gas emissions. The collapse of biodiversity continues. Socio-political tensions keep erupting. Scientific reproducibility is largely incongruent with the property of complex systems to generate emergent properties which are inherently unique and not reproducible. It is also incongruent with changes in complex systems with severe consequences that harm humanity and life on the earth.

Traditional science claims to be value-free and objective-verified by tests and experiments which prove or disprove its validity. Observer effects are therefore anomalous and should be eliminated. This is first-order science, or *exo-science*. There is a newly emerging science which is challenging these assumptions. In its nascent form it appeared on the scene some six to seven decades ago in the emergence of cybernetics.[5] Although it appeared as a fringe perspective, it has spun off some major dislocations to traditional knowledge and has influenced key aspects of the technology which is now ubiquitous on the planet, including computational systems, artificial intelligence and social engineering. However, these aspects of cybernetics have generally been taken over by the first-order perspective to such an extent that is necessary to define a second-order cybernetics.[6] This is providing some of the principles of second-order science, or *endo-science*.[7] The second-order paradigm proposes that the researcher (observer) is included in the world of investigation; therefore, his or her world-views, expectations and motives are an inseparable component of the knowledge created. The state of the observer is crucial to the kind of truth that might be discovered. Put another way, a key instrument of scientific inquiry in turbulent times is the scientist him- or herself.[8]

The left-hand diagram shows the traditional science viewpoint with the observer outside the system. The second diagram on the right shows the second-order viewpoint where we now include the observer inside the system.

In an exploration of the seeming dichotomy between theory and practice, an interdisciplinary group of scientists, practitioners and policy-makers spent three days largely in dialogue around the following question: 'How might second-order science improve the way that policy is created and applied?'[9] After a series of dialogues around different subsidiary questions, a distillation was made to formulate what a comprehensive constitution of second-order science will be like. Many elements of this are already present in current practice, albeit in a piecemeal way. Even some aspects of first-order science depend on one or more of these components functioning even though they remain undiscussed by the mainstream.

This exploration follows seven threads which interweave in various ways depending on the emphasis of the exploration. The components are first presented separately as seven threads. To conclude this chapter, ideas on how they weave together to enhance our ability to deal with hyperturbulence are discussed.

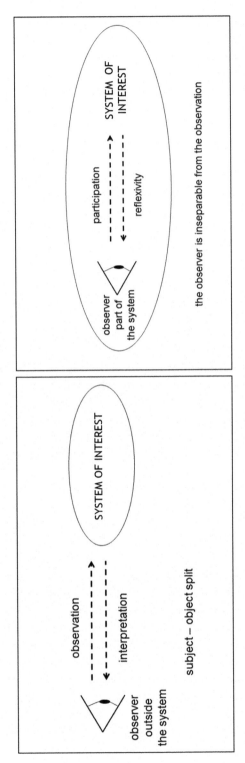

Figure 2.1 From first-order to second-order systems

Thread 1 – presence of the observer

'In no way shall the observer enter into the observation'[10] is one of von Foerster's aphorisms summarising the nature of first-order science. This view claims to generate 'objective knowledge' about the 'real world' out there. On this basis the scientific endeavour has vastly expanded our known universe and provided a knowledge platform for the growth of technology into every aspect of life. The requirement in this paradigm to exclude the observer, the scientist as person with awareness, leaves out those aspects of life which are not reducible or containable in the confined rules of engagement of first-order science. This absence is a key factor reducing our effectiveness in the face of global complexity and turbulence.

Viewed from the point of view of consciousness all scientific knowledge is a form of intersubjective consensus amongst a community of scientists. Where those scientists are ignorant of their assumptions about knowing, they are restricted by second-order blindness to the implications of their position. However, the observer is also a decider and an actor and, in that sense, imposes policy by the very nature of the way he or she frames observation. The presence of the observer in the observation is a condition of the nature of second-order science. More fundamentally the centrepiece is not the observer alone but the triadic system of observer, society and language. The *observer* is participating in a *society* with a *language* that makes communication about the matter at hand possible. To have any one of chicken, egg and rooster is insufficient – it is necessary to have all three.

Heinz von Foerster, referring to Socrates, said, 'He knows that he knows nothing; that is an initial condition of knowledge; but many do not know that, and that is a condition of second-order ignorance'.[11] In that sense all reflection is, by definition, second-order wisdom – the wisdom of consciously not knowing. One of the most valuable aspects of second-order science is the sharing of the experience of partial knowledge, multiple perspectives and acknowledged ignorance of the question we are trying to understand. This is not a position readily taken in a first-order culture that demands specialised expertise and 'right answers'. This position is part of the challenge in creating the new paradigm.

A transdisciplinary exploration of second-order from a variety of perspectives and backgrounds opens up a rich discussion which has a dual nature of progressing various lines of enquiry at the same time as it is raising considerable frustration in the search for clarity of shared definitions and language. This seems to us to be entirely consistent with opening up a developing field and being on a 'learning journey',[12] which itself is a second-order endeavour.

The structural and circular nature of the field as contrasted with the linear sequential nature of linear logic is more like breaking into the circular loop and exploring the space. This is also in the spirit of von Foerster's definition of second-order cybernetics as 'the study of observing systems'.

Implications for systems research and practice

Hyperturbulence faces us with undecidable questions. If the observer is excluded then the ethical response to the challenge of undecidable questions generated by hyperturbulence are excluded. This predicts a response of following existing rules which lack the requisite variety and a breakdown of trust.[13]

Thread 2 – observation, intervention and ethics

The observer is not merely an observer. Observation is an aspect of enactive cognition in which the embodiment of the observer is crucial. The meaning of observer needs extending with terms like actor, decider and intervener. From an enactive second-order perspective, in a world that is highly structurally coupled, there can be no such thing as a totally detached observer. Structural coupling occurs whenever there is a history of recurrent interactions which forms a congruence between two or more systems (Maturana & Varela, 1987). Any position (even that of seeming non-observation) can be an intervention. In human experience indifference can be devastating. For example, the seemingly objective nature of high energy physics served by massive infrastructures like the Large Hadron Collider is the result of an intersubjective consensus between hundreds of scientists and politicians to privilege that kind of research through massive investments and to make claims for that view of the world.[14] Dominant fields of science are now embedded in substantial infrastructures of shared data, shared technological facilities and shared modalities and expectations of what constitutes science.

In such structures assumptions are being made based on values and judgements as to what is 'in' and what is 'out' of consideration. Yet these judgements are often invisible and remain unquestioned. Research becomes a subjective game played on a field where the game itself is taken as objective. However, the implications are such that each dominant infrastructure is itself an intervention in prescribing the accepted nature of science. This can be correlated with Kuhn's distinction[15] between science that is puzzle solving (within a field) and science that is paradigm shifting (disrupting and changing the field itself). This leads to a clash between socially constructed boundaries and natural boundaries, usually with unintended consequences. Part of the second-order process needs to involve developing a shared language of values and ethics. Midgley[16] emphasises that the modality of second-order science is intervention rather than observation in its passive, detached sense. This moves science on from simple inquiry into truth to also supposing rightness. If it can be done, it should be done. First-order science is not actually value neutral whatever its claims to the contrary. Thus intervention implies considering boundaries as an essential second-order discipline to reveal what are often limiting assumptions in bringing about change in society – again with implications for policy.

An implication for policy is that the use of 'objective evidence' is at risk of being interpreted and used as an argument for political ends without making clear the value assumptions behind its 'objectivity'. A complementary second-order discipline would seek to make clear the position assumed by the 'objectivity' of the research.

Implications for systems research and practice

For a more effective response to a hyperturbulent situation it is important to view everything, including passive not-doing, as action which may carry ethical implications. Approaching this consciously greatly improves the capacity of the actor to respond to conditions of hyperturbulence.

Thread 3 – reflexivity and reciprocity

Observation and intervention are not one-way streets. There is reciprocity between the observer and the world observed. The observer is participating, and there are consequences. Making the observation may not leave the observed unaffected. This is well acknowledged in the uncertainty principle in quantum physics. Second-order science takes this as a condition of all observation, albeit with very different scales of registered effect. Reflexivity adds the power of the observer being able to observe the act of observation[17] and reflect on its implications. It is reciprocity with consciousness, which has implications for policy-making. First-order policy interventions tend to assume a problem situation needs fixing, apply a fix and then assume alleviation of the problem. There is no change in the nature of the system intervened in. However, intervention often creates new conditions (sometimes referred to as unintended consequences), for example by provoking new ways of gaming the system. A second-order policy would pay much more attention to this effect and as a result would have to be adaptive to emergent conditions.

Implications for systems research and practice

Given the emergent and undefinable nature of hyperturbulence, any actor in the situation has to be able to adapt and learn not just at the single-loop level but also at the double-loop level. That is to say assumptions have to be constantly questioned and criteria adjusted. The absence of reflexivity renders this impossible. Also, both the conditions and the responses will be in an ecology of other actors where decisions of any actor will affect the position of other actors. This is more likely to be in balance if there is reciprocity.

Thread 4 – circularity and re-entry

It is well known in the domain of first-order systems modelling (Morecroft, 2007) that effects can be causes (causal loops). Second-order circularity implies feedback from the observation that changes the condition of the observer. One interpretation of this is the idea of the observer as a learning system. A more technical version is the principle of re-entry – that any field can be applied to itself as, for example, theory of theory, method of methods and cybernetics of cybernetics. From a second-order perspective the observer is continuously bringing forth a world and responding and learning from that world. This stance supports the view that complete comprehensiveness is impossible. Knowledge is not some static object 'out there' but is constantly reforming through the engagement of the knower; and the knower is changed by the encounter with knowledge.

Implications for systems research and practice

In hyperturbulence the objects of the previously seemingly stable world (the eigenforms) no longer hold. New rapidly repeated experiments are essential to discover new eigenforms which bring a different level of stability to the actors. In balance, eigenforms are let go of before they outlive their usefulness. This condition can also be described as ultra-stability.

Thread 5 – reflection and perception

We are used to the practice of reflection in the sense of mentally looking repeatedly some piece of knowledge we have taken on board or generated. Second-order science takes this further and treats the self-experiencing mind as the primary conscious instrument of the science, *a priori* to the tools of investigation and measurement – microscopes, telescopes, computer modelling and so on. This shows up in the idea of a science of qualities drawing on the tradition, parallel to Newton, advocated by Goethe.[18] The perception of qualities requires acknowledgement of the human presence in the perception as the sensitive detector of quality. The science of qualities, therefore, participates in the attributes of second-order science and should, in my view, embrace this approach as complementary to that arising from second-order cybernetics. An important aspect of this approach is its emphasis on the unique nature of a given human observation capable of attuning to and making sense of distinction as contrasted with mathematical average. Reperception also opens up the territory for creativity which is an essential human requirement for navigating hyperturbulence.

Another aspect of the human mind that is essential for generating new knowledge is creativity. This is essential for the progress of first-order science but is often rationalised out of any account. The creative observer is removed from the novel observation in the process of 'scientific reporting'.

Implications for systems research and practice

In a fast-changing, hyperturbulent environment it might be thought that reflection was simply not available since there are no gaps in the demand for action. However, the opposite is the case. Without reflection the actors will tend to project the last moment's perception pattern onto the emerging situation and misinterpret it. So a rhythm of reflect, perceive, act, reflect is necessary.

Thread 6 – transdisciplinarity

On the one hand first-order science has built its structure of knowledge through intense cultivation of specialised disciplines which develop their own methodologies, language and ways of explaining the world. Even when disciplines interact to form cross-disciplines (such as biochemistry, astrophysics and complexity science) these tend rapidly to assume the same bounded status as other disciplines. On the other hand the world shows up in richness and complexity such that any discipline is a slice through a greater reality. In second-order science the direction is towards greater inclusiveness and the search for common cross-cutting principles. In this respect interdisciplinarity only goes so far since it is the juxtaposition of existing disciplines. Transdisciplinarity is an attempt to go under and beyond these distinctions and seek other forms of insight.

Implications for systems research and practice

This principle is also connected with requisite variety in that specialised depth will lead not just to blind spots but whole areas of blindness. The actor who can, through experience, through advice or teamwork cover a wider variety of perspectives on a situation and integrate it through holistic thinking will be better able to adapt.

Thread 7 – multi-perspective dialogic

In dealing with complex situations that do not yield to a single discipline it is valuable to take several perspectives. This principle was successfully applied in the early days of operational research. The principle is recursive in that, even within a discipline, multiple experts may bring out different aspects and enrich understanding. The practice of seeking a second opinion is well used and the same applies in this sense to peer review within a discipline. Second-order science takes this further since it assumes the reflexive and generative nature of inter-subjective consensus building. The process of dialogue around a question from a number of disciplinary or stakeholder perspectives enables a creative emergence. Peer review can become enclosed and self-serving.

Flanagan[19] emphasises the idea of third phase science. The terminology of three phases rather than two orders (first and second) may seem confusing at first. My own framing of this distinction is that second- and third-phase science are both forms of what here is called second-order science. The distinction is that in third-phase science the multi-observer dialogue is an essential procedure of the discipline. This type of emergent process is also reflected in Wahl's account of a science of qualities. Emotional coherence[20] is needed, not just intellectual synthesis.

Multiple perspectives, brought together, are important for discovering blind spots. However, information itself is not enough. Unless there is participation there will not be understanding and ownership by the different parties. Situations that seem intellectually coherent will disintegrate for value and emotional reasons that have not been worked through. A second-order dialogic process acts as stabiliser ensuring greater acceptability.

Implications for systems research and practice

Rather like reflection it may seem that there is no time for dialogue and that command and control is a more secure basis for rapid and timely action. This may be true in sub-sectors of activity in terms of implementation. However, without a shared appreciation of the overall pattern of changes, responses and their consequences, this will lead to fragmentation and reduce adaptive response. Dialogue in the preparation for hyperturbulence shows its value in a shared action language across the multiple needed perspectives.

Weaving the threads

These seven shared attributes of second-order science are summarised in Figure 2.2. In this representation the explicit presence of the observer is made the central distinction. Sharpe[21] points to the irreducible nature of

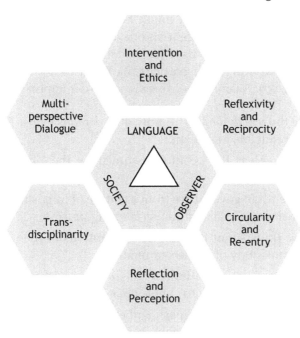

Figure 2.2 A seven-fold structure for a complete second-order science

the first-person experience. If we accept this, all knowledge is seen as some form of intersubjective co-ordination of our first-person experiences of the world. The first-person perspective is, of course, prominent in many of the social sciences. Umpleby[22] points out that in the social sciences knowledge is not just the product of an investigation but also part of what is investigated. Some approaches in the social sciences include several of the factors in the summary diagram above and partake of second-order perspectives. He also points out that 'an overly limited conception of science (i.e. one that excludes the observer and the effects of theories on society) limits investigation and constrains how science can contribute to improvements in society'.

In Figure 2.2 the core essential condition of second-order science is the central triangle of observer, language and society. The six outer attributes may be more or less strong in a given piece of second-order work. For example, some research strongly emphasises re-entry. Other research emphasises transdisciplinarity. Yet other research makes reperception and creativity a major factor. These differences are partly to fit the method to the requirement but also partly due to the fragmentation of the field. A strong second-order science would weave these strands together to mutually reinforce one another. The essential points for policy development in a world of hyperturbulence are summarised here as a speculative indicator of what the benefits of such an interwoven approach might be. There are parallels here with action research which is "emergent and developmental. It concerns practical issues and human flourishing. Its modality is primarily participative and democratic, working with participants toward knowledge in action." (Bradbury, 2015, p7). A comprehensive second-order approach might

1   appreciate the real dynamics of individual persons whose future behaviour is not reducible to statistics;

2   seek to make clear the position assumed by the 'objectivity' of the research;

3   stimulate a shift in governance from a culture of imposition to a culture of experimentation as a continuous learning process;

4   make more transparent the hidden assumptions in the use of models by a re-entrant study of models of models;

5   take far greater notice of individual differences through qualitative methods and shape policy to enable greater self-organisation;

6   take a transdisciplinary approach and ensure a much wider incorporation of knowledge and judgement from different fields;

7   adopt a second-order dialogic process, different from customary consultation, to act as stabiliser, ensuring greater acceptability through participation and multiple contributions.

The simplistic application of policy can result from decision-makers not having the time, means, or interest to hear multiple sides of issues before choosing. If decision-making does not establish an inclusive, transparent and coherent means of reflecting policy deliberations on complex situations, policy deliberators are at risk of losing their public legitimacy. This is a huge social risk of unintended consequences and backlash clearly pointed out by Ulrich:

> There is a need for a simultaneous revision of the contemporary concepts of professional competence and of citizenship. Professional practice and the practice of citizenship need to be understood in such a way that professionals and citizens can meet as equals, though not necessarily as equally skilled individuals. [23]

This, however, will require an introductory form of second-order science that is both readily intelligible and translatable into practice. This requires the involvement of the public, of communities of interest as well as experts and politicians. New forms of collaboration between all stakeholders are required to get the voice of all perspectives into the dialogue. Stakeholder analysis sheds light on the range of perspectives which influence or will be influenced by a specific policy deliberation, and an even representation of all perspectives will provide a mechanism for discovering the nature of the dilemmas seeking resolution. This dilemma identification – and potentially additional alternative definitions of related problems – then must be taken to a larger forum for ratification on an inclusive and transparent basis.

The central issue of deciding what action to take in the face of contingent uncertainty and hyperturbulence is also a political issue, and such a decision can only be taken by reaching beyond observational science and accessing broad civic aspiration. The technology for merging matters of concern with matters of fact is an emerging science, and this aspect of second-order science does not have precedents in established observational science disciplines.

A working hypothesis to move this forward is to affirm that decisions are more likely to accord with the realities it is trying to govern if it actively applies the seven attributes to the research and development of policy in an integral way – weaving the threads together.

From this analysis we propose a set of guiding principles. Involve those who will need to enact the policy at the start and recognise their observations of the issues in the situation of concern and recognise that for each situation a new language has to be crafted. Recognise 'policy as learning' and therefore a process of learning cycles. Realise that in a situation of circular causality, sorting the situation out 'head-on' is likely to have significant unintended consequences. Create conditions for those involved to have a safe context in which they can share observation and learning without sanctions and where 'learning from mistakes' is part of the process. Whatever the focus of the policy area, do not restrict participation to specialists in that area alone. Place the policy-making in a wider context. Use processes of facilitated dialogue and similar methods to ensure that 'all voices are heard' and that prior persuasions do not overly restrict what is allowable and what is off-limits. Even where the policy has a foundation in what seems to be 'hard' evidence, consider the ethics of any policy position as part of its evaluation.

Having affirmed this view, it is important to retain clarity that advocacy for a second-order approach is not intended to displace or contradict first-order science – rather to enhance its possibilities and place it within a more human- and value-determined context. However, what the second-order perspective does is open up a better way to integrate the relationship between the past-oriented, evidence-based decision-making and the future-oriented foresight basis of decision-making. This requires nothing less than a reperception of the nature of the future. This is the topic of the next chapter.

Notes

1 Morin, E. (1999). *Seven complex lessons in education for the future*. Paris: UNESCO.
2 Page, G., Wise, R., Lindenfeld, L., Moug, P., Hodgson, A., Wyborn, C., & Fazey, I. (2016). Co-designing transformation research: Lessons learned from research on deliberate practices for transformation. *Current Opinion in Environmental Sustainability*, (20), 86–92.
3 Fazey, I., Schäpke, N., Caniglia, G., Patterson, J., Hultman, J., Mierlo, B., . . . Wyborn, C. (2018). Ten essentials for action-oriented and second order energy transitions, transformations and climate change research. *Energy Research and Social Science*, *40*, 54–70.
4 Steffen, W., Richardson, K., Rockström, J., Cornell, S. E., Fetzer, I., Bennett, E. M., . . . Sörlin, S. (2015). Planetary boundaries: Guiding human development on a changing planet. *Science*, *347*(6223).
5 E.g. Pias, C. (Ed.). (2016). *Cybernetics – the Macy conferences 1946–1953: The complete transactions*. Chicago: Chicago University Press.
6 Scott, B. (2004). Scott 2nd order cybernetics: An historical introduction. *Kybernetes*, *33*(9/10), 1365–1378.
7 Muller, K. H., & Riegler, A. (2016). Mapping the varieties of second-order cybernetics. *Constructivist Foundations*, *11*(3), 443–454.
8 Naydler, J. (1996). *Goethe on science: An anthology of Goethe's scientific writings*. Edinburgh: Floris Books.
9 Müller, K., Flanagan, T., Midgley, G., Wahl, D., Hämäläinen, T., Lähteenmäki-Smith, K., . . . Getz, L. (2017). 'Second Order Science and Policy'. Edited by Anthony Hodgson and Graham Leicester. *World Futures* 73, no. 3 (2017).
10 von Foerster, H. (1995). Ethics and second order cybernetics. *Stanford Humanities Review*, *4*(2), 308–319.
11 von Foerster, H. (2014). *The beginning of heaven and Earth has no name, complexity/design/society 21*. New York: Fordham University Press. p. 26.
12 O'Hara, M., & Leicester, G. (2012). *Dancing on the edge: Competence, culture and organization in the 21st century*. Axminster: Triarchy Press.
13 von Foerster, Ethics and second order cybernetics.
14 Boisot, M., Nordberg, M., Yami, S., & Nicquevert, B. (Eds.). (2011). *Collisions and collaboration: The organization of learning in the Atlas experiment at the LHC*. Oxford: Oxford University Press.
15 Kuhn, T. (1962). *The nature of scientific revolutions*. Chicago: University of Chicago Press.
16 Midgley, G, and Ochoa-Arias, A. E. (2001). Unfolding a theory of systemic intervention. *Systemic Practice and Action Research*, *14*(5), 615–649.
17 See Bortoft, H. (2012). *Taking appearance seriously: The dynamic way of seeing in Goethe and European thought*. Edinburgh: Floris Books. p. 13.
18 Naydler, J. (1996). *Goethe on science: An anthology of Goethe's scientific writings*. Edinburgh: Floris Books.
19 Flanagan in *Second order science and policy*.
20 Flanagan, T., & Lindell, C. (2018). *The coherence factor: Linking emotion and cognition when individuals think as a group*. Charlotte, NC: Information Age Publications.
21 Sharpe, B. (2010). *Economies of life: Patterns of health and wealth*. Axminster: Triarchy Press.
22 Umpleby, S. (2014). Second-order science: Logic, strategies, methods. *Constructivist Foundations*, *10*(1), 16–23.
23 Ulrich, W. (2000). Reflective practice in the civil society: he contribution of critically systemic thinking. *Reflective Practice*, *1*(2), 247–268. [ISSN] 1462–3943 © 2000 by Carfax Publishing/Taylor & Francis Ltd.

Chapter 3

Reperceiving the future

Step 3 – First glimpse of the ox

The 'glimpse' makes an impact; it encourages and inspires us to continue on the search.

Seeing the tracks is not enough. We need to achieve glimpses of the direction in which our desired insights lie. The glimpse that grew on me was an inkling that the way we are culturally conditioned to regard space and time is a constrained interpretation of our experience. Taking the future seriously through techniques like scenario planning seemed a step in the right direction, but they are still constrained by the presuppositions of linear time. Another constraint emerges from the deterministic world-view which forbids any influence on the present from the future. Whereas the requirement works for the influence of the past on the present, usually assumed to be causation, there is no space for causation from the future. The future does not exist and therefore we have no evidence from the future.

If we suspend the deterministic world-view, it leads us to the interesting proposition that the insights we seek to correlate with the new hyperturbulent circumstances need to be so different from our current ones that perhaps they are, in some sense, located in the future. To detect them in the future we need to cultivate a capability for future consciousness. This anticipatory capacity we have in a small way or else we could not navigate our daily lives, but we are not used to exercising and developing this capacity at a larger scale for seeing what has to be done to achieve a new state of affairs in the more distant future. Yet future consciousness in its basic form is a capacity to perceive the future in the present.[1] Through this exercise we develop our capacity for anticipation.

Modern physics and cosmology have identified anomalies which open up and question the prevailing assumptions. For example, non-locality, or 'spooky action at a distance', challenges the assumption that causation takes place only through conventional space and time. Some phenomena at the quantum level are interpreted as action from the future. Of course, these are taking place in the quantum world, not in the zone of our direct experience.

Another example is the emergence of uncertainty as a fundamental condition of the world, coupled with complexity and chaos. Extrapolation from the past and present into the future requires a machine world-view in which knowing the mechanism allows projecting its behaviour at some future time. Whereas this is true for some aspects of the world, it simply does not extend to cover it all.

For direct experience we need to take a phenomenological approach. This builds on our acceptance that the presence of the observer is acknowledged; therefore, how we experience space and time is itself valid evidence for what their nature might be. We begin to see the future differently.

This is the third stage of ox herding.

~~~~~

Changing boundary perception

Moving over to the second-order viewpoint of systems science now enables us to open up the question of how we view the future and what role future thinking needs to play in a world of hyperturbulence. One way into this is through ideas stemming from Gerald Midgley's systemic intervention approach.[2] A primary goal of systemic intervention is the improvement of the system in question. The definition of 'the system in question' is often itself a function of agreement amongst multiple stakeholders and is not simply a fixed object 'out there' as is first-order science. The negotiable ambiguity of the system in question requires choosing what is considered the boundary of the system. Boundary critique can be helpful in clarifying the ambiguity and the power dynamics around agreeing what the system is that is to be improved, and for whose benefit. I will describe some essential features of systemic intervention.

For a given situation, *systemic* means attending to wholes, connectedness and non-linear behaviour, with a special emphasis on boundaries concerning who and what is included, excluded or marginalised. Intervention means purposeful action by an agent to create change, so systemic intervention, therefore, means purposeful action, incorporating reflection on boundaries, aiming to bring about some improvement.

The diagram in Figure 3.1 represents a simple, basic form of boundary critique for a single stakeholder, or where agreement between multiple stakeholders has been reached on what is in and what is out. The outer broken line determines the boundary between what is perceived as relevant to the intervention and what is considered irrelevant. The inner broken line represents the negotiated agreement as to the system in question, which is subject to the intervention. The peak represents the 'centre of gravity' of the sense of identity and underlying values that make the system in question meaningful. In the case of stakeholders in contention, it would be necessary to use several of these diagrams with differing degrees of overlap.

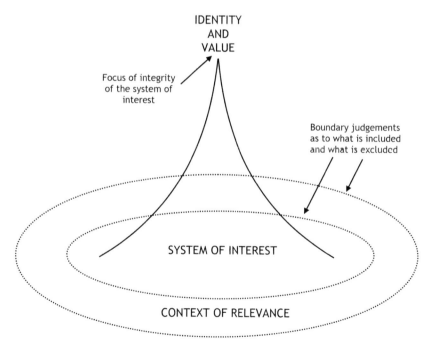

Figure 3.1 The basic concept of boundary critique

The boundaries represented in this exposition are essentially about content, and tend to be spatial and semantic in character; who or what is included or excluded. Mapping boundaries helps to surface assumptions and clarify agreement about what is in and what is out of the system in question. We now take this further and add the dimension of time within the boundary critique concept.

To relate time to the systems idea it is necessary to go beyond the simple linear, sequential view of time (short, medium and long term) (Hodgson, 2017). This is especially true where the situation of interest is going through transformative change. We need to consider the qualities of the temporal window of interest by distinguishing between the kinds of systemic improvement that have a sustaining role and those which have a transforming role, as shown in Table 3.1. Negotiating hyperturbulence needs intense periods of transformative change; sustaining change is inadequate.

Shifting to a new pattern requires some form of strategic thinking and foresight.[3] I will describe the various disciplines of foresight and futures studies using a framework introduced by Bill Sharpe.[4] Foresight can be classified into four types according to the extent to which the decision-maker has agency to do things and the degree of uncertainty they are facing. This distinction classifies four basic modes of futures methods, as shown in Figure 3.2.

If the decision-maker has relatively low agency, for example when managing in a stable-going concern operating in a relatively stable and certain environment, the classical methods of forecasting followed by resource planning in relation to those forecasts can be effective. These methods generally assume a predictable world where, for example, the measurement of past trends can be extrapolated into the future without any problem. The limitation of these methods is that they assume the continuity of a fundamental pattern with perhaps minor incremental changes. Innovation will tend to be dominantly reinforcing the status quo. Such orientation is quite

Table 3.1 Comparing transformational with sustaining change

Sustaining Improvement	Transformational Improvement
Supporting and reinforcing the current dominant pattern	Shifting to quite a new pattern with transformed fit to a radically different context
Relatively restricted specialist viewpoint on 'systems in question'	Wide angle view of the 'system in question', taking a holistic approach
Innovation that is captured to prolong the status quo	Disruptive innovation which renders the status quo obsolete

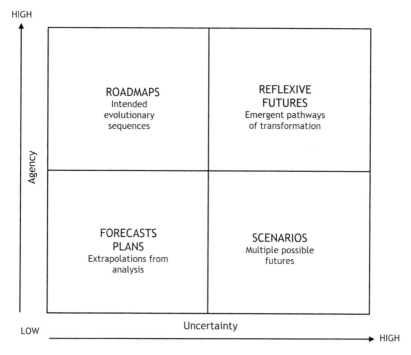

HIGH

Agency

ROADMAPS
Intended
evolutionary
sequences

REFLEXIVE
FUTURES
Emergent pathways
of transformation

FORECASTS
PLANS
Extrapolations from
analysis

SCENARIOS
Multiple possible
futures

LOW

Uncertainty

HIGH

Figure 3.2 Four modes of foresight

inadequate in the face of hyperturbulence and clearly will lack the necessary adaptive or anticipatory capacity.

If the decision-maker has high agency in a relatively stable and certain operating environment, as for example when implementing successive generations of products in an established manufacturing enterprise, the method of road maps into the future applies. The strategic plan is based on successive generations of products with additional market appealing features.

If the decision-maker has high uncertainty but low agency, the preferred method of considering the future is the development of multiple scenarios. No single scenario is a prediction but rather a 'what if?' possibility. A set of, say, four scenarios can cover a range of uncertainty. The challenge to the decision-maker is then to seek a resilient strategy that has a chance in each scenario, although with different tactics. Or it is to realise that a choice has to be made biased towards one scenario where the others become the basis of contingency planning.

In forecasts, road maps and scenarios there are buried assumptions about the nature of time. Consider the example of a strategy based on an analysis of trends, aiming to reach a certain goal over a time span in which the trend is still valid. There are two levels of looking at this – the linear and the sophisticated. The linear is most common and held in place by the cognitive difficulty people have in visualising trend bends driven by nonlinear dynamics, for example exponential curves. The sophisticated version does take into account nonlinear trends but still places them within a presumed stable environment. Faced with a situation of hyperturbulence, then, this continuity view of time leads to conclusions that can be far off the mark in a turbulent environment. I believe this is not only a technical problem of method but also a philosophical and sociological problem of how we view the nature of time. This is not abstract, since material consequences follow from it, one of which is to explore the nature of anticipation, the topic of the next chapter.

Generally we take for granted without noticing that the future exists without questioning the nature of its existence. Since we work with the notion so extensively, it must surely exist in some form or another. But in what sense does the future exist? There are a number of viewpoints here in the dominant economic and management cultures. There is certainly no single agreed-upon viewpoint.[5] The subconscious viewpoints we hold on the nature of the future have a strong effect on what we value, what we consider significant and what we act upon.[6] They affect our methods, practices and results. What might have worked in relatively stable conditions ceases to be helpful in the face of turbulence. We need to dig deeper into answering the question of what we are really dealing with here as the future if we are to transform our adaptive capacity. We cannot gain a new understanding of the nature of the future when we treat it from the same framing we use with material things existing in the past from where we can gain evidence, verify by experiment and generally apply a scientific method. We cannot pin down 'evidence from the future' in this way, so foresight, however methodical, must differ from being a science in the first-order sense.

Although our common language tends to treat 'the future' as something that exists, we make it an object of study, as in 'future studies'. But there are many possible angles on this existence. The future does not seem to exist as the present exists, so it could merely be an abstraction, a mental construct that is useful to considering choices. It could have the stronger role of being a depiction of possibilities or an image of a future that might be desired, avoided or adapted to. The future might also be a convenient illusion, giving the impression that we can affect and change it. On the other hand the future might be a set of possibilities beyond the current status quo with different likelihoods of coming to pass, for example sea level rise as a result of global warming. A challenging interpretation that I have been particularly interested for several decades is that our conventional model of time as past, present and future is itself deeply flawed and actually we are dealing with a complex, multi-dimensional world in which there are possibilities that, in some wider sense of to 'exist', the future does exist and can affect the present. Perhaps there are event horizons that can be seen by incorporating human other ways of knowing including intensified consciousness, intuition and creativity into the means of study and perception.

Alongside these considerations is also the question of method, of the way in which we study the future. If we believe that the future unfolds pretty much based on the past and present, we study causation, trends and cycles and extrapolate them into the future. If we believe that the future is not necessarily a continuum, we look for possible trend breaks, discontinuities and breakdowns. These may be unpredictable or, like economic bubbles, predictable. The unfolding of the future may not be linear, so we may use systems models to simulate complex behaviour with emergent properties and see what happens. Images of the future depend on recognizing plausible (and even implausible) patterns that give shape to a future state of affairs. Faced with obscurity in the future, a kind of 'future fog', we can use imaginary worlds as hypotheses or we can extrapolate inevitable consequences that might be invisible to most people.

The hyperturbulent environment of today challenges human organisations to maintain a span of attention that can sustain the resilience and adaptability needed for surviving and thriving. This span of attention is in both space and time. This span is called the present moment. In Figure 3.3, the circles represent the sphere or domain of a self-determined purpose.

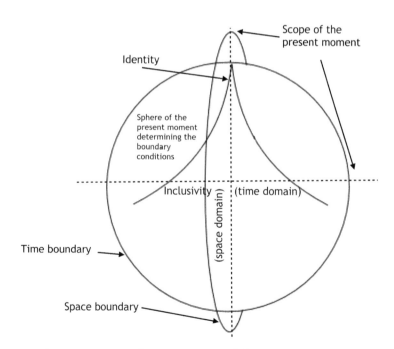

Figure 3.3 Boundary critique and the present moment

This may be individual or social.[7] Since interests are complex and overlap, there are actually multiple circles with multiple boundaries[8] of which the diagram is a general picture. The horizontal and vertical dashed lines represent the scope of the present moment. The present moment is the way we represent the experienced phenomenon of the scope and content of the domain of interest. That is partly determined by our direct experience of duration and the systemic boundaries that define the domain. The full-on circle represents a time span of interest in the more conventional sense; the perspective circle represents spatial content or stuff of the present moment.

The present moment is characterised by the complex *pattern* of entities, processes and causal relationships embodied in it and is also characterised by its own *dynamic environment* which is an essential concept to avoid falling into the trap of fixed images of time. Within this whole area, causality is not a simple linear property but complex and multi-dimensional. This model echoes the notion of Aristotle of the four types of cause[9] namely material, formal, efficient and final.

Anticipating the unpredictable

In a turbulent environment that is characterised by the high agency / high uncertainty character represented in the top right quadrant of Figure 3.2, how could it be possible to anticipate emerging futures? Poli points out that anticipation implies a shift in the paradigm of causality.[10] It especially needs the recognition of latency, that a situation can be open and with hidden aspects. The concept of latency or potential is a crucial component of the elaboration of the present moment. Latency relates to the experience of perceiving potentiality for being; that which is latent has the possibility of coming into being in time. Poli also makes the distinction between explicit and implicit anticipation. Explicit anticipations are those of which the system is aware. Implicit anticipations work below the threshold of consciousness, for example an instinct to be in the right place at the right time.

Even though the environment is constantly changing in unpredictable ways, this does not rule out the possibility of anticipation. For this to be possible there has to be openness to different inputs to the present moment and a role for creativity. Jay Ogilvy reinforces the condition of openness of the present moment with the idea of the 'scenaric stance', which is able to hold contradictory possibilities and space for creativity.[11] It must be emphasised that the 'scenaric stance' is not quite the same as defining multiple scenarios mentioned earlier. It represents

> a new approach to the future, a new attitude toward time. Neither ahistorical like the ancients, nor optimistic like progressive modernity, nor

present mystic like the post-modernists, this new approach will hold in mind at once both the high road and the low road, and acknowledging the possibility of either, and giving full weight to human will in determining which path we actually take.[12]

This way of looking at the future requires us to rethink our capacity to embrace permanent ambiguity and to put our faith in *acting in an anticipatory way in the present*. It implies a recovery of a world-view enabling the creative openness of our experience. Riel Miller sums up the implications of this: 'The perpetual ambiguity of Ogilvy's "scenaric stance" calls on us to live the novelty that defines each instant of the re-assembling present[13] – at once inherently novel and closed – until the next moment'.

The anticipation in the present moment[14] implies four conditions of mindfulness. Multiple futures, not necessarily compatible, are held in the consciousness of the present. Future consciousness is open to the presence of choice and creative action. The mind must be capable of being steady in its embrace of this openness and complexity – responsibility for choice in the face of undecidable questions[15] of the unfolding future.

Decision-makers face a fundamental dilemma between the sure leadership of sticking to a justifiable strategic course and the unsure leadership of changing course in the face of little tangible evidence in the conventional sense. How do you do due diligence in the face of needing to commit to radical change in a context of high uncertainty? The decision-maker is challenged to consider alternative futures to the usual assumptions that are not understandable at the level for commitment, because they require a significant shift in both the mental models and the attitudes of the decision-maker. A facilitator has the task to help the decision-maker experience the needed repatterning and reframing, which internalises a new future to the intensity of action.

It is interesting that, in the foresight disciplines, there is still relatively little methodology for the reflexive futures area, where both agency and uncertainty are high[16], yet this is the area which is increasingly the hyper-complex operating environment for government, commerce and society more generally. This necessity, for example in the challenge of climate change, is stimulating approaches[17] which tackle the paradox of finding structures to understand better how to act in the unstructured.

Reflexive futures can be characterised as strategic exploration. The high agency component of the decision-making is reflected in a practice of setting a strong vision of a future state of affairs in which the actor is occupying a desired position (much as Ackoff recommends in his interactive planning[18] systems approach). The uncertainty component of the decision-making is treated in qualitatively different time zones, each with its own dynamic. By qualitatively different we mean features like the differences between predictive, transformative and emergent ways of framing the future. The method of *three horizons*[19] has been developed specifically to provide a practical means of tackling the challenges of the fourth quadrant.

At the core of this is the development of a multi-dimensional future consciousness that integrates scanning and logic with the capacity to see into the future through different lenses of awareness in the present moment.

The three horizons

The three horizons method was introduced into government foresight in 2006[20] and has since spread amongst strategists and policy-makers.[21] Its applications are particularly useful as a context for transformative innovation[22] in business and the public sector, especially health care.[23] It has also been used at scale, for example, in the conference Transformations 2017 held at the University of Dundee. Facilitation practice applying this method has been codified to help practitioners by H3Uni, an innovative not-for-profit.[24]

In Figure 3.4, the line labelled Horizon 1 represents the viability in a given context or environment of the current dominant pattern or structure of the system in question. Its viability is considered to be degrading because of an increasing mismatch with the changing external conditions. The line labelled Horizon 3 represents a different transformed pattern which, although seemingly with minor significance early on, turns out to be a much better fit with the changing external conditions and becomes the dominant viable pattern. The line labelled Horizon 2 represents the turbulent, even chaotic, situation of transition from one pattern to another. An example of this is disruptive technology, which may stimulate both creative innovation and resistance in equal measure until the technology becomes normal.[25] It is often not culturally feasible in real-world business environments (because of conservative attitudes, sunk investments etc.) to jump straight to Horizon 3 early on, when the strategic fit appears low. For this reason, compromises are made and a turbulent tension is experienced between competing pressures to conform to Horizons 1 and 3. The resulting trajectory is represented by Horizon 2.

The three lines in the figure, taken together, unfolding over time, represent three potential futures. In particular circumstances, Horizon 1 may prevail by sustaining innovation that merely reinforces the status quo. An organisation may strongly push its 'success' formula, not realising that it is out of date, and may ultimately overshoot its relevance and collapse (Sterman, 2000). This is what happens when companies resist hearing the 'bad news' that more radical change is needed. In other circumstances Horizon 3 may prevail, when a farsighted company spots a change in the environment and moves wholeheartedly to align with it, even if this means lower profits in the short to medium term. This is not the most usual reaction to

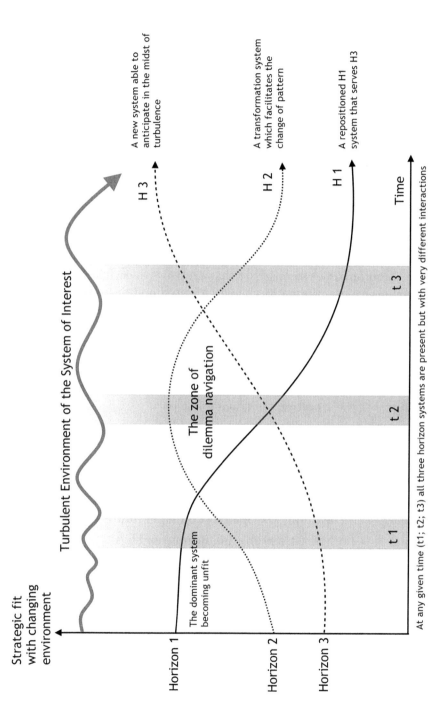

Strategic fit with changing environment

Turbulent Environment of the System of Interest

A new system able to anticipate in the midst of turbulence

H 3

A transformation system which facilitates the change of pattern

H 2

A repositioned H1 system that serves H3

H 1

Time

The zone of dilemma navigation

t 1   t 2   t 3

Horizon 1

The dominant system becoming unfit

Horizon 2

Horizon 3

At any given time (t1; t2; t3) all three horizon systems are present but with very different interactions

Figure 3.4 The three horizons of future consciousness

accepting the importance of change, however. More often, companies find themselves on a bumpy Horizon 2 trajectory, as they seek to chart a strategic course that keeps stakeholders on board who are advocating both Horizons 1 and 3. So Horizon 2 represents a turbulent but not sudden transition.

Note the way the lines are drawn such that they are all present in any given slice across the time axis. By way of clarification, this can be thought of in three stages. At t1 the H1 'business as usual' world is dominant but beginning to fail; H2 innovation is on the ascendency. H3 is still a fringe possibility often discounted or unnoticed. At t2, H1 is already in serious decline; H3 is noticed and is beginning to attract resources that displace H1, and the innovation in H2 is generating a high variety of experimentation. At t3, H3 has become the dominant paradigm now, much more fit for purpose than H1. Importantly, H1 has not gone away. Essential elements are maintained but in a different role, often more related to basic infrastructure. H2 is calming down as H3 is stabilising the new pattern. Of course, in the fullness of time and with constant change, H3 will become the new H1.

Table 3.2 summarises some of the characteristics of each horizon.

H2 requires two transformative changes – from simplistic to complex thinking and from static to dynamic thinking. First we'll look at complex thought.

Table 3.2 The characteristics of each horizon

Horizon 1 policies and rules	
Based on	expertise – so glued to the past
	specialisation – so inevitably fragmented and linear
	individualistic power of the few over the many – so lacking social justice
Horizon 3 requirements	
Increasing	learning – so open to a different future
	holistic – so able to integrate and heal
	collaborative – so able to achieve intelligence beyond the individual
Horizon 2 navigation	
Transforming by	regeneration – recovering lost integrity, nature and humanity
	systems understanding – finding transformative structures
	co-creation – participative creativity finding new needed patterns

The primary role of the three horizons is to facilitate repatterning of perception. This is a psychological step in futures thinking characterised by Pierre Wack. Burt[26] describes Wack's view of three factors that determine the way we interpret the future. The first is the 'macroscope' – the wider, complex, interconnected system in which the organisation exists. The second is the identification of inter-related actions – complexes of driving forces that generate systemically inevitable events. The third is our prevalent mind-set. Stepping out of the assumption trap requires a shift from being caught in a mind-set to taking on new perspectives of 'what if'. Wack describes this mental repatterning with the word *reperception*. The distinction here is that we take mind-set to be a fixed pattern in contrast to adopting a perspective which can be contrasted with other perspectives.

A decision-maker, challenged to step out of his or her mind-set, is actually more complex than just an observer; he or she is a *participant*. To take a decision is to commit to some interaction with the field of the decision and bring forth a world. From a systemic point of view, the decision-maker is an integral component of the decision systems he or she works within and is partially determining the future.[27]

Hyperturbulence can only be navigated in an *anticipatory* manner that acts on intuitions beyond the status quo. Reperception is an intuitive act to shift the mind to see with different 'internal eyes' and pick up signals from the future that would otherwise be missed. Creativity and imagination are closely related to reperception.[28] Induction is another way of interpreting reperception. A crucial aspect of this is the recognition of anomalies; things which don't fit the usual set of assumptions and taking the trouble to notice them and take heed[29] of their implications.

Reperception can be recognised as a creative act in the context of entrepreneurial activity. The entrepreneur is not only reading possible futures differently from the mainstream but also imagining how to make the future turn out differently from what is generally expected. There is a 'make a new future happen' component. This is not independent of insightful reading of the environmental trends. Successful new enterprises often are led by people who see a wave of the future coming but modify it by 'surfing' the wave with new products or services. For them, that future is now, but it has not yet been unfolded and distributed.

Deepening the paradigm shift

Reperception can also be seen as a necessary response to the emergence of a new paradigm as defined in Chapter 2. A paradigm designates the fundamental categories of intelligibility[30] of our world and controls their use. Individuals are patterned how to know, think and act according to these interiorised culturally inscribed paradigms. In other words, the paradigm has a strong emotional and subconscious power that holds people to a dominant belief system. In Morin's words:

> The paradigm is both underground and sovereign in all series, doctrines, and ideologies. The paradigm is unconscious but it irrigates and controls conscious thought, making it also super-conscious. In short, the paradigm institutes primordial relations that form axioms, determine concepts, command discourse and/or theories. It organises their organisation and generates their generation or regeneration.[31]

The formulation of the global challenge as one of hyperturbulence is itself the overture to a paradigm change. The proposition I am making in this chapter is that such a change in understanding needs not only seeing the content of the situation differently but also seeing the nature of time itself differently. To provoke this paradigm shift we introduce two additional time-like dimensions.[32] Although there are arguments from physics that can support this approach its basis is phenomenological reflection on experience.[33]

This changes the way we can consider the question 'what do you mean by the future?' To represent this extended view of time we use John Bennett's method[34] of using one of the three dimensions of space to represent conventional chronological time and the two remaining spatial dimensions to represent two additional time-like dimensions. To get beyond the habitual associations we have with the words 'time' and 'future' we introduce Greek names referring to experience rather than mathematical theory. The use of Cartesian dimensions is used as an analogy to aid visualisation.

The three time-like dimensions are chronos,[35] aionios[36] and hyparxis,[37] as shown in Figure 3.5. At the centre is the total set of immediate mental objects that constitute the conscious experience of the present moment. The horizontal dimension refers to the way the content of the present moment, in the form of traces, memories, expectations and hopes, creates the span of time, the sense of duration. The vertical dimension represents the latency in the form of active patterns and appearance as passive forms. The diagonal dimension, or z-axis, represents what we might call living commitments entering from the past but differently from causal time. It also represents, intriguingly, influences from choices not yet made but held in mind. Table 3.3 defines their meaning as we use them here.

Associated with the idea of dimensions of time is also the idea of the *qualities* of time. Since the common interpretation of time is so clock-bound, it is better to describe them as 'time-like dimensions'. A challenge to describing this idea comes from two seemingly contradictory prevalent views. There is the 'common sense' view, also supported by the majority of physicists, that time's arrow travels only in one direction (from past to

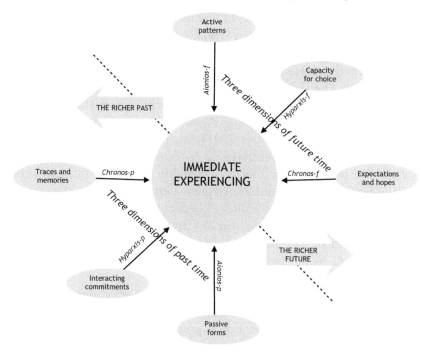

Figure 3.5 The multi-dimensionality of the present moment

Table 3.3 The three time-like dimensions

Greek Term	Description
chronos	time on the move; time as before and after; measurable time; experience of duration
aionios	enduring pattern; without beginning or end; lasting an age; potential in the present
hyparxis	realised potential; ableness to be; non-causal manifestation; capacity to bring about; coming into being

future). The contrasting view of a minority is that common sense time is an illusion and there is no flow.[38]

Within our experience there can also be moments where consciousness gathers itself in whilst refining the intensity and embrace of the present moment. This intensity reveals the confluence of different influences on now to a moment of immediate significance. This may be an internal realisation or an external synchronicity of events. The Greek term useful to this experience of pattern in time is kairos; we refer to the 'kairos moment'. The kairos moment catches a fulcrum of change, a transformational shift. It is a synchronous moment where the whole explains the parts in contrast to the dominant culture which attempts to explain the whole from its parts.

In the multi-dimensional view, influences enter the present moment from the future. The richness of the present moment is a function of the extent and quality of the different types of influence. Each dimension is an influence entering and enriching the now. To visualise this we need to suspend the convention that time flows from left (past) to right (future) and consider the dimensions as converging to 'now' at the centre. The spatial axes *x*, *y*, and *z* by analogy enable us to visualise that these influences come into the present from these different dimensions. In Figure 9, all the arrows point *into* the sphere of the present and impact the mental experiential content. In more conventional terms, three of the incoming influences are past-like (including linear time, labelled chronos-p) and three of the incoming influences are future-like including future influencing the present (labelled, chronos-f).

Conventional time is experienced through the traces and memories in the mind that imprint the present from the past. Retro-causality, whether imaginary or real, is experienced as expectations and hopes. The passive form of *aionios* is the presence of relatively enduring forms. The active side of *aionios* is the vast superposition or multiple presence of possible patterns and states. The *hyparchic* past is the sense of meaningful dynamic or interacting commitments that still prioritise in the present. The *hyparchic* future is the region in which the present moment is open and evokes choices and decisions. Thus there are six sources of insight that can contribute to future consciousness, and they can be deliberately incorporated into practice.

An anticipatory system capable of navigating hyperturbulence has a modelling function which is able to carry out time path mapping faster than the unfolding of 'real' time.[39] The impact of the output of this internal modelling on the behaviour of the system is not to be confused with feedback, which is information from the past about deviation or error from a set norm. In contrast, information from anticipated future states is essentially a *feedforward* process. This feedforward capability is also implicit in the Conant Ashby principle that any regulator of a viable system needs to incorporate a model of its own system and its environment.[40] Anticipation implies deciding what to do now in this present moment in terms of what is perceived to be the consequence of that action at some later time than the immediate now and in radically changed circumstances. Feedforward requires the system to have the capacity to model the world in such a way as to estimate future developments powerfully enough to actually commit to what seems to be imprudent (e.g. betting the firm). Feedforward may also emerge as a cybernetic consequence of intuition.

An anticipatory system is able consider decisions as open rather than constrained in an algorithm. Open decisions arise in the face of questions that are undecidable,[41] a situation typical of hyperturbulence. There are no algorithmic precedents. Decisions are fundamentally second order in nature.[42] Open decisions are a key component of navigation, which weaves together understanding of the decision field with the decision process and the wider range of five influences beyond time past, namely time future, dominant forms, latent patterns, living commitments and open creative indications.

So far in the search we have identified the 'ox' as standing for a different way of seeing the world that might be more congruent with the emerging global circumstances of hyperturbulence. We have taken one promising approach to be that of systems thinking in its broadest sense However, seeing systems from a first-order, reductionist perspective does not seem adequate. We need to move to a second-order view – that the presence of the observer must be acknowledged and the implications of this taken into account, including additional and different ways of knowing.[43] We saw some emerging tracks of the ox. This is not sufficient for navigating hyperturbulence. We need to anticipate the future in new ways. The introduction of second-order perspective opens up to the importance of reframing our notions of time and dimensionality in order to step out of the deterministic linear view, which is simply one perspective. Reperceiving the nature of time and dimensionality opens up new possibilities for understanding anticipation. This is gaining a first glimpse of the ox. We may be able to pick more information as to what is about to happen from a wider bandwidth.

The next chapter takes this foundation and explores the nature of a different kind of system – the anticipatory system.

Notes

1 See Sharpe, B. (2013). *Three horizons: The patterning of hope*. Axminster: Triarchy Press.
2 Midgley, G. (2000). *Systemic intervention; philosophy, methodology, and practice*. New York: Kluwer.
3 Miller, R. (2007). Futures literacy: A hybrid strategic scenario method. *Futures, 39*(4).
4 Sharpe, B., Fazey, I., Hodgson, A., Leicester, G., & Lyon, A. (2016). Three horizons: A pathways practice for transformation. *Ecology and Society, 21*(2), 47.
5 Dator, J. (2017). Editorial: Time, the future, and other fantasies. *World Futures Review, 9*(1), 5–16.
6 Staley, D. (2017). Time and the ontology of the future. *World Futures Review, 9*(1), 34–43.
7 Ackoff, R., & Emery, F. E. (1972). *On purposeful systems: An interdisciplinary analysis of individual and social behaviour as a system of purposeful events*. New York: Transaction Publishers.

8 Midgley, G. *Systemic intervention; philosophy, methodology, and practice.* New York: Kluwer, 2000.

9 Material cause: 'that out of which'.
   Formal cause: 'the account of what is to be'.
   Efficient cause: 'the primary source of change'.
   Final cause: 'that for the sake of which a thing is done'.
   Falcon, A. (2012). Aristotle on causality. In *Stanford Encyclopedia of philosophy.* Stanford: Stanford University. Retrieved from http://plato.stanford.edu/archives/win2012/entries/aristotle-causality/

10 Poli, R. (2010). The many aspects of anticipation. *Foresight, 12*(3), 7–17.

11 Ogilvy, J. (2011). Facing the fold: From the eclipse of utopia to the restoration of hope. *Foresight, Emerald, 13*(4), 7–23.

12 Ogilvy, loc cit.

13 The term 'reassembling present' refers to the dynamic and even transformative possibilities within the present moment. Miller also refers to this as openness to a creative future rather than a predicted one. Miller, R. (2007). Futures literacy: A hybrid strategic scenario method. *Futures, 39*(4).

14 Hodgson, A. (2018). Second order anticipatory systems. In R. Poli (Ed.), *Handbook of anticipation.* New York: Springer.

15 von Foerster, H. (1995). Ethics and second order cybernetics. *Stanford Humanities Review, 4*(2), 308–319.

16 See Harkins, A. M., & Morovec, J. W. (2011). Systemic approaches to knowledge development and application. *On the Horizon, 19*(2), 127–133. Grim, T. (2009). Foresight maturity model: Achieving best practices in foresight. *Journal of Future Studies, 13*(4), 69–80.

17 Levin, L., & Hampel, S. (2017). *Future stewards: Leading new ways to counter climate change.* Retrieved from https://leadersquest.org/content/documents/Future_Stewards_summary_2016-2020.pdf

18 Ackoff, R. (1981). *Creating the corporate future.* Chichester: Wiley.

19 Sharpe, B., Fazey, I., Hodgson, A., Leicester, G., & Lyon, A. (2016). Three horizons: A pathways practice for transformation. *Ecology and Society, 21*(2), 47.

20 Curry, A., Hodgson, A., Kelnar, R., & Wilson, A. (2007). *Intelligent infrastructure futures.* London: Foresight Office of Science, UK Government. Sharpe, B., & Hodgson, A. (2006). *Towards a cyber-urban ecology: Intelligent infrastructure futures technology forward look.* London: Office of Science and Technology.

21 Curry, A., & Hodgson, A. (2008). Seeing in multiple horizons. *Journal of Futures Studies, 13*(1), 1–20.

22 See Leicester, G. (2016). *Transformative innovation: A guide to practice and policy.* Axminster: Triarchy Press.

23 Leicester, G. (2018). *SHINE: Changing the culture of care.* Aberdour, Scotland: International Futures Forum. Retrieved from www.iffpraxis.com/tih-shine-case-study

24 www.h3uni.org/project/facilitate-3h-mapping/

25 Christensen, C. M. (1997). *The innovator's dilemma: When new technologies cause great firms to fail.* Cambridge, MA: Harvard Business School Press.

26 Burt, G. (2010). Revisiting and extending our understanding of Pierre Wack's the gentle art of re-perceiving. *Technological Forecasting & Social Change, 77*, 1476–1484.

27 Umpleby, S. (2007). Reflexivity in social systems: The theories of George Soros. *Systems Research and Behavioural Science, 24*, 515–522.

28 Markley, O. (2012). Imaginal visioning for prophetic foresight. *Journal of Future Studies, 17*(1), 5–24.

29 Holland, J. H., Holyoak, K. J., Nisbett, R. E., & Thagard, P. R. (1986). *Induction: Processes of inference, learning and discovery*. Cambridge, MA: MIT Press.

30 Morin, E. (1999). *Seven complex lessons in education for the future*. Paris: UNESCO.

31 Morin, loc cit, p. 9.

32 Hodgson, A. (2013). Towards an ontology of the present moment. *On the Horizon, 21*(1), 24–38. Hodgson, A. (2016). *Time, pattern, perception: Integrating systems and futures thinking* (PhD thesis). University of Hull. Retrieved from www.academia.edu

33 Hodgson, A. (2019). Foresight and the seven dimensions of experience: A transdisciplinary transcultural approach. *World Futures, 75*(3), 113–134.

34 Bennett, J. G. (1966). *The dramatic universe* (Vol. 4). London: Hodder and Stoughton.

35 **chronos**: time on the move, time as before and after, measurable time.

36 **aiónios:** agelong, eternal pattern, unending, lasting an age, totality.

37 **hyparxis**: realised being, ableness-to-be, manifestation, capacity to bring about.

38 Cullender, C. (2014). Is time an illusion? *Scientific American, 23*(4), 14–21.

39 Louie, A. H. (2013). *The reflection of life: Functional entailment and immanence in relational biology*. Dordrecht: Springer.

40 Conant, R., & Ashby, R. (1970). Every good regulator of a system must be a model of that system. *International Journal of Systems Sciences, 1*(2).

41 von Foerster, Ethics and second order cybernetics, 308–319.

42 Hodgson, A. (2010). Decision integrity and second order cybernetics. In S. Wallis (Ed.), *Cybernetics and systems theory in management: Tools, views and advancements* (pp. 52–74). Hershey: IGI Global.

43 Rajagopalan, R., & Midgley, G. (2015). Knowing differently in systemic intervention. *Systems Research and Behavioral Science, 32*, 546–561.

Chapter 4

Anticipatory systems are different

Step 4 – Catching the ox

At this stage, changes in world-view are inevitable; one begins to lose attachment to official explanations of all kinds and starts to explore unofficial views.

To incorporate systems, observers and futures I believe we need to take a step from the mechanistic to the organismic view of nature. Much resource has been put into trying to explain life by the mechanisms of physics and chemistry. A great deal of that mind-set has taken root in 'rational' approaches to socio-political understanding. Yet we see the momentum of misunderstanding continues to drive the unfolding drama of the Anthropocene.

If the world is not simply a mechanism, what is it? A mechanism is something made of components that can be assembled and disassembled. Any overall function of the mechanism is seen to be derived from the assembled, interrelated functions of the parts. The primary tool of understanding is analysis. The function of the whole can be inferred from its bits, which can stand in their own isolation. Everything of interest can be measured and quantified. The machine is seen to be independent of the observer, even though this view tunes out the fact that even machines arise from purpose.

Systems thinking attempts to step beyond this mechanistic view to an organismic viewpoint with such statements as 'the whole is greater than the sum of the parts', 'effects can be causes' and 'systems can be self-producing'. Further, qualities of wholeness become significant, not just their quantities, but in their qualities. This becomes evident only if we are willing to adopt a second-order perspective, where we recognise that knowledge emerges in consciousness. As we proceed from physics to biology and then go further to human society, we see the aspect of meaning has to be considered. Purpose, the fourth cause of Aristotle, has to be considered. We are dealing with purposeful or teleological systems. Purpose tends to be excluded from the mechanistic view, even in systems thinking.[1] What is the purpose of any given system?

Now an interesting thing about purpose is that it refers to something, some state, in the future. It points in a direction of both functional change and increased meaning.[2] If we take the view that a system can be purposive and it is that which distinguishes it from a mechanistic system, what kind of a system is it? The proposition made here is that it is an anticipatory system which is responsive to influences from the future as well as adaptive responses to the past. Further, this future responsiveness is operating in a much richer space-time continuum where there is more than one 'dimension' of the future. This qualitatively richer continuum has also within it scope for spontaneity and creation and is only partly bound to the momentum of what we conventionally call 'the past'. I take the elusive 'ox' to be the possibility of an *anticipatory present moment*. It is a property of a system at the human level in which consciousness plays a key role.

This is the fourth stage of ox herding.

~~~~~

Foresight as anticipation

A substantial challenge in practicing futures thinking with decision-making is that, in decision science, we are used to shaping decisions analytically on existing evidence, whereas foresight requires thinking beyond the evidence. Usually decision-makers and futurists live in different paradigms that are incongruent if left unchanged. Systemically this leaves foresight only weakly coupled with execution.[3] However, if decision and foresight are cybernetically coupled, there is a two-way influence which can set up an *anticipatory system*,[4] a concept developed by Robert Rosen. From a strategic decision-making perspective, our interest in the future is to anticipate it sufficiently to take advantage of opportunities and be better able to avoid threats.[5] Anticipatory systems thinking challenges us to go beyond current methods of foresight and futures studies and also beyond the usual decision-making processes.[6] The idea of anticipatory systems emerged from considering the nature of life in biological systems. So what is the idea of an anticipatory system?

An anticipatory system has a modelling function which is able to carry out time path mapping faster than the unfolding of 'real' time.[7] The impact of the output of this internal modelling on the behaviour of the system is not to be confused with feedback, which is information from the past about deviation or error from a set norm. In contrast, information from anticipated future states is essentially a *feedforward* process. This feedforward capability (perhaps more accurately feed-from-forward) is also implicit in the Conant Ashby principle, that any regulator of a viable system needs to incorporate a model of its own system and its environment.[8] Anticipation implies deciding what to do now in this present moment in terms of what is perceived to be the consequence of that action at some later time than the immediate now[9] and in radically changed circumstances. Feedforward requires the system to have the capacity to model the world in such a way as to estimate future developments powerfully enough to actually commit to what may seem to be imprudent (e.g. betting the firm). Feedforward may also emerge as a consequence of intuitions of future conditions.

Dealing with ambiguous situations necessarily involves the actor or observer. However, first-order reductionism leaves out the observer. A second-order cybernetic approach to anticipatory systems includes the observer. Since anticipation incorporates the capacity to act in accord with as well as perceive the future (or some representation of it), from a second-order perspective, the state of the observer is a key factor in the functioning of an anticipatory system. This accords with the nature of second-order cybernetics.[10] the core of which is an inseparable triadic network of observer, society and language (see Chapter 2).[11] The nature of that triadic network is a second-order anticipatory system which is now described in four stages.

First, the first-order perspective on the anticipatory system is outlined and amplified by a second-order perspective; second, a brief description of relevant second-order science is outlined; third, the transdisciplinary ingredients for constructing a second-order anticipatory system are proposed; finally, a conjecture regarding the structure of a second-order system is introduced as the anticipatory present moment (APM).[12]

Poli, in his review of the many forms of anticipation (Poli, 2010), points out a fundamental issue in considering the nature of systems which are, in some way, able to anticipate the future. In what sense is the future there to be 'made use of'? Considering this question from a second-order observer perspective requires a link between the nature of systems that function within a temporal order and the phenomenology of time-consciousness: how are we aware of the future? To accommodate this question, Rosen's definition needs expanding in a way that offers the possibility of integration with the phenomenology of the present moment.

A necessary aspect of an anticipatory system is feedback in which effects are causes. A feedback loop will feed into the present of system information regarding past behaviour of the system, which clearly can be of value in adjusting its present behaviour. However, if the only information feeding back into the system is from the past, it does not sufficiently meet the criteria for anticipation. It is necessary that the system be able to adapt its behaviour through incorporating information from the future. This requires a repatterning of the basis of decision and action, which is likely to appear incongruous to the past-oriented evidence based mind-set. The simple term Rosen (1985) used for this additional loop is feedforward. The conventional interpretation of this feature is that the system operates with models of possible futures that go beyond those constructed simply from past information.

Rosen's idea that an anticipatory system is one which contains an internal predictive model of itself and its environment goes beyond a reactive system based solely on feedback. Reactive systems can only respond to changes that have already happened and, to be effective, depend on a repeated environment or context. In contrast, an anticipatory system not only responds this way but also takes into account futures that have not yet happened – the 'not yet'.

From first-order to second-order anticipatory systems

A second-order development of the anticipatory system includes as part of the system an observer who is able to reflect and act on the consequence of anticipatory model assumptions. This opens up the possibility of creativity and acausal factors entering into the decisions of the system.

Figure 4.1 presents an extended version of Rosen's anticipatory system. In the diagram, S stands for system, which may be an individual organism, an ecosystem, or a social or an economic system. At first view, S is an ordinary non-anticipatory dynamical system. M represents a model of S. In Rosen's account[13] the behaviour of S is considered to be taking place in conventional real time. The behaviour of M, however, is taking place in a time variable which goes faster than real time. This means that after a fixed interval T then M will have proceeded further along its behavioural

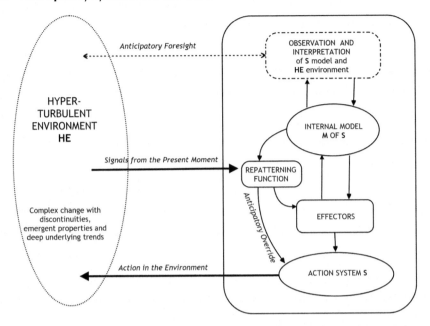

Figure 4.1 Second-order extension of Rosen's anticipatory model

trajectory than S. In this way, the behaviour of M predicts the behaviour of S; by looking at this stage of M at time T_1 we get information about the stages that S will be in at time T_2. M and S are set up to interact in specific ways. Suppose system M is equipped with a set E of effectors which allow it to operate either on S itself or on the environmental inputs to S, in such a way as to change the dynamical properties of S. The whole system will now be adaptive such that prospective future behaviours determine present changes of state. Anticipation would require the further property that M can discriminate between desirable and undesirable states and can change the dynamics of S in a way to avoid the undesirable region as well as cope with mutual possible trajectories in the future.

If S is a planning system, we can make further propositions from this model. To be anticipatory beyond adaptability, the system needs to be open to interactions that enable M to be revised and extended beyond inherited experience (feedback), and the system needs M to be able to reframe and re-perceive its advance running in the light of an anomalous situation that is not yet experienced (feedforward). There is also the question as to whether, without openness to information from the future and in some sense 'guessing futures', the system is fully anticipatory in an impredicative world in which time may be richer than simply a linear 'block time' future.

From a second-order perspective the case can be made that such anticipation is facilitated by the reflexive nature of an observing system which is able to ask itself what its view of the future is. In first-order science the notion of anticipation is problematic because of what has been summarised as 'the zeroth commandment', that future states cannot affect present changes of state. In second-order science the nature of time and causality are open to reframing, so the possibility of a theory of anticipation is more plausible.[14] Especially important in this view is the concept of inferential entailment in mathematics, which is considered to correspond to forms of enactive relationship in biology as described in the emerging field of relational biology,[15] in which relational modelling emphasises integration rather than mechanistic reduction.

Louie considers that this 'information from the future' is not actually from the future but is information about self, species and the evolutionary environment encoded in the organisation of living systems. This is the idea of model-based behaviour, where the model can contain aspects that are speculated future states, not directly derivable from past causality. Having said that, Louie (2010) also makes a strong case for the admission of the 'forbidden' concept of teleology to legitimately re-enter science.[16] Discussing this in the context of the Aristotelian four causes, he points out that three of them (material, efficient and formal) are congruent with Newtonian physics but the fourth, final cause, is conventionally rejected. However, the Newtonian paradigm itself violates the existential nature of time and therefore cannot be regarded as an adequate comprehensive frame for considering what is scientifically acceptable.[17] The extension of dimensions beyond space-time leaves open more radical ways to consider what the future is that is being used in anticipatory systems.[18]

Taking a transdisciplinary viewpoint

What is time? The ontology of time in philosophy has been largely concerned only with an ill-defined instant or with a timeless 'eternal now'. The question needs broadening out. An ontology of all present moments, including past and future states is needed.[19] We can begin from our experience of the present, the actual 'now'. What exists in the human mind is our present moment, and this can be different according to the state of our consciousness. Our attention to the present can be constricted with very little content or it can be very expansive with a multiplicity of impressions informing it. In the ordinary way, experience is of the content which is being actualised coupled with its traces of the past and expectations of the future. Within that personal present moment, freedom is limited by the commitments of the past and recognition of latent patterns of potential. If the commitments are high and the recognition is low, the present moment is a conditioned state in which the self has little power of choice. This is one version of the 'thin' present moment. It is, however, possible to transcend this conditioning by abandoning attachment to the current content of the present moment, expanding the consciousness and thereby experiencing a larger present moment with more degrees of choice and freedom. This is the 'thick' present moment. A sentient human walker resting at the bottom of a valley can, unlike a rock, bring to mind the destination over the hill and climb out – still conditioned by the physical situation but exercising freedom to transcend it. This is due to the fact that the processes 'inside' the walker are not wholly determined by the contextual processes of its environment, as is the case with the rock.

The present moment in some way contains aspects of the future – future-in-the-present. Containing the future in some existent way implies the idea that the future can influence the present in a distinct way beyond any modelling function such as is proposed in first-order anticipatory system theory. The status of both the present and the future are not the same in this context as in the conventional timeline of past, present and future. In this alternate view, the key framing is a topological one of nested present moments of different scales of present moment. This means that what is contained in a larger present moment can be in the future of a smaller present moment. This is another way of interpreting that some 'saw it coming', whereas many did not.

In Figure 4.2 the present moment of a system is represented by a circle of which a time span is a diameter. In present moment theory the future

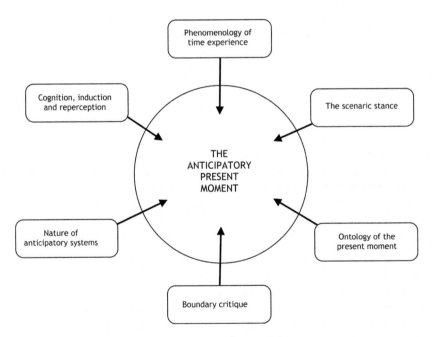

Figure 4.2 Six concepts composing the anticipatory present moment

exists: but it does not exist within a small, conditioned 'thin' time slice. It exists in a greater 'thick' time slice. Our future is not-yet-now for us, but it is already present as a latency. We cannot say that the future is 'in' the future in a linear sense. What we can say is that an event that is substantially in our future is already present in a larger present moment. The notion of present moment also implies sentience. This may be of differing degrees depending on the level of reality in focus.

The conjecture made here is that a systemic structure of a second-order anticipatory moment can be constructed from the integration of the following six aspects depicted in Figure 4.2.

The APM brings together the following perspectives, clockwise from the top:

- the phenomenology of time experience;
- the scenaric stance towards the future;
- the ontology of the present moment;
- boundary critique as a second-order notion;
- the nature of anticipatory systems;
- meta learning through varieties of reperception.

These aspects are described briefly in the following sections.

1 Husserl's model of time consciousness

Husserl developed his theory regarding the problem of the continuity of the perceptual present in contrast to the conventional idea that now is a 'thin' present between the future and the past. Instead he saw it as a 'thick' present.[20] For example, if we are listening to a note played on an instrument we hear it as a continuous duration. When we are part way through, the sound of the first second is no longer audible. In terms of our experience, however, it is still a present tone that we are hearing. The meaning of the tone in, say, a musical work, is also evoked in relation to its future ending.

The immediate experience of the earlier part of the sound is not the same as a memory of that sound. There is a distinction between *retentions of experience* and memories of that experience. The present future of the sound is *protention* as an extended present. The idea of a knife-edge present, or a thin instant, is abandoned. Retentions are qualitatively different from memory reproductions in that they are all part of the current consciousness of the present. Protentions also contain elements of the emergent proximate future, which can be distinguished from fantasised futures. The present moment thus contains elements of conventional past and future, experienced as an extended now as in Figure 4.3 (Gell, 1992).

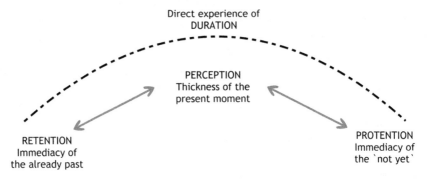

Figure 4.3 Representation of Husserl's account of present experience

2 *The basic nature of anticipatory systems*

The phenomenology of the present as the properties of retention, perception and protention serves to integrate anticipation in a reflexive way. It is necessary to extend the basic concept of feedback as applied in adaptive systems. A feedback loop will feed information into the present of a system regarding past relationships of the system, which has limitations of value in adjusting its present behaviour to an unknown future. It is necessary that the system also has the property of feedforward in order to be able to adapt its behaviour to be ready for the 'not yet'.

As previously stated, an anticipatory system needs a way that information regarding the future can be acquired. One way is that an anticipatory system contains a predictive model of itself and its environment, which enables it to make choices which are not entirely based on past information. Another way is that in some sense, aspects of the future already exist and therefore an anticipatory system can have the additional capacity to pick up information regarding the future, which is neither inferential nor based on a predictive model; 'using the future' could include perceiving an existent future. This requires two distinct channels of information input as shown in Figure 4.4, one from the past retention side and the other from the future protention side.

3 *The ontology of the present moment*

The 'beingness' of the present moment is a crucial aspect of the APM.[21] The essential features that need to be borne in mind for synthesis are recapitulated here. Poli's distinction between a thin and a thick present moment supports the idea that the present should be considered an extended duration that interfaces between the past and future, which is in contrast to its being a knife-edge between the past and the future. The thickness of the

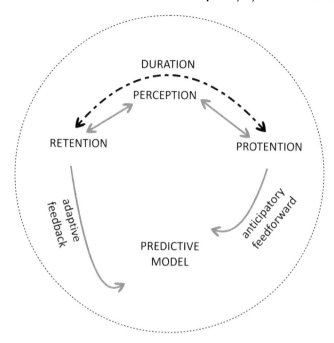

Figure 4.4 A phenomenological view of anticipation

present moment is related to a sense of dimensionality that is both mea-surable, in the sense of dimensionality in physics,[22] and phenomenologi-cal, as in the Husserlian and Bergsonian notion of duration. Bennett (1966) extended this interpretation to six dimensions of experience: namely traces and memories, interacting commitments, passive forms, active patterns, expectations and hopes and capacity for creative decisions. This idea of the present moment was introduced earlier in Chapter 3, Figure 3.5.

4 The structure of boundary critique

The notion of boundary critique in systemic intervention addresses prob-lematic situations with second-order reflections on boundaries. This was described earlier at the beginning of Chapter 3. Consideration of a present moment implicitly assumes or defines the scope of a boundary in time. Psychologically this is determined by both the duration of attention and concern over time and the richness or variety of the content under consider-ation. A present moment is complex, non-linear and generative of emergent properties, including those influenced by the future. The boundaries of a system are defined by the limits of the knowledge that is taken as pertinent to the system in question.

In considering human systems as anticipatory systems, then, boundary critique can supply a rationale and method for supporting not only clarification of the system in question but also the present moment in which that system is being considered. This idea of the boundary critique was introduced earlier in Chapter 3 Figure 3.1.

5 Cognition and perception

The decision-maker is actually more than just an observer. To take a decision is to commit to some interaction with the field of the decision and 'bring forth a world'. An investment decision depends on financial resources in the decision system potentially at the disposal of the decision-maker. Although observing and analysing the situation, from a systemic point of view the decision-maker is an integral component of that decision system. Markets are reflexive to the decision-makers who participate in them. How people play a market affects the behaviour of that market.

We need also to understand both feedback and feedforward in terms of inductive learning. As described by Holland and colleagues[23] the key trigger for induction is anomaly. Inductive learning is taking place stimulated by information from the past or previous experience. This is hard enough, but the challenge of induction in the anticipatory system is dealing with anomalies that have little or no basis in information from the past. Usually we are 'future blind' in this respect. A falling 'leaf' is seen to behave in a self-propelled way from flower to flower provoking a reinterpretation as 'butterfly'. But in a world where we have never seen self-propelled plant seeds (as in the movie Avatar), how do we anticipate such and adjust beliefs and behaviour accordingly?

Stated as a paradox, the important distinction here is that anticipation needs the capacity to imagine the unimaginable and see the invisible.[24] Entertaining multiple representations of a possible reality that has not yet happened is one way a system can become anticipatory. This is a challenge to cognitive and perceptual capabilities.

6 The scenaric stance

This refers back to Ogilvy's notion of the scenaric stance introduced in Chapter 3. That is the simultaneous entertaining of multiple scenarios of the future that may be contradictory (for example, both pessimistic and optimistic) and leaving room for the unknown and the creative. This frame of mind is also clearly consistent with opening to anomaly and contradiction, which can support anticipation. To practice this we need a capacity to embrace permanent ambiguity and to put our confidence in acting in the present, but with a greatly enriched multi-dimensional experience of the present moment.

Reperceiving as described by Pieree Wack[25] or repatterning is necessary to allow for the creative openness of our experience. This orientation
accords with the 'open future' that is part of the present moment concept,
with this future being imagined within an enlarged (or 'thick') present.

The structure of the anticipatory present moment

A challenge in understanding the notion of the anticipatory present
moment as an integrated concept is that it is embedded in a second-order
perspective, meaning it is a concept of a *system with consciousness*. In terms
of our experience it is related to how we intentionally structure our experience to take advantage of the latent powers in our mental and emotional
intelligence. The experience of the present moment is a practice of mindfulness that integrates with the way our brain and nervous system can be
programmed. It is both a structure and a discipline. The rest of this chapter
will concentrate on structure, but the role of awareness must be taken into
account as it will in Chapter 7.

The key notions which underpin this synthesis between systems thinking, futures thinking and consciousness are

- multiple futures, not necessarily compatible, held in the consciousness
  of the present;
- openness in that consciousness to the presence of choice and creative
  action;
- capacity of the mind steady in its embrace of this openness and
  complexity;
- the implications of responsibility for choice in relation to the unfolding
  future.

These support the integrating concept of the notion of the present moment
put forward here.

The figure depicts the APM. This diagram requires some unpacking.

The circle represents the scale and extent of the present moment in
question. It also represents the selection or identification of the relevant
boundary conditions. The momentum entering the circle on the left represents the influences of conventional pattern of causation from the past
of this particular present moment. The expression 'locked in' signifies, as
an example, the tendency of organisations to become, in changing conditions, victims of their own success. The anticipation exiting the circle on
the right represents the influence of information from the future enabling
transgression of the locked-in pattern that is better suited to emerging
conditions. This is exemplified by organisational leadership, which is able

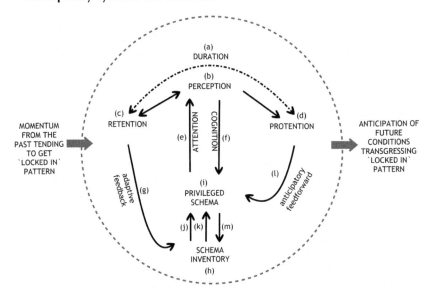

Figure 4.5 The systemic structure of the anticipatory present moment

to break out of the historical pattern of success and adventure into new forms. The present moment in question is recognised as the experiential or phenomenological aspect of the self-agency of the system in question. This second-order observing self is taken to include a cognitive system represented by the components within the circle. The alphabetical tags on the diagram reference to components of the diagram to the descriptions which follow.

The different components of this diagram are labelled (a), (b), (c) and so on. These aid the referencing to the diagram in the description that follows. Subsidiary perspectives of the diagram are given in Figures 3.4, 3.5 and 4.1. The main components are:

a)   Duration – the fundamental experience of time consciousness;
b)   Perception – what is seen to be present;
c)   Retention – the active retrospective present;
d)   Protention – the immediate sense of the future;
e)   Attention – the directing of interest;
f)   Cognition – the mental sense making of the moment;
g)   Adaptive feedback – adjusting to information from previous experience;
h)   Schema inventory – the set of mental interpretations available in the mind;

i) Privileged schema – the selected interpretation of the moment (the dynamic repatterning function);

j) Promotion of schema from past – recovery from previous history;

k) Promotion of schema from present – immediate interpretations of current 'reality';

l) Anticipatory feedforward – alertness to information from the dimensions of the future changing the basis of schema selection;

m) Promotion of schema from future – innovative interpretations not extrapolated from accumulated experience – the anticipatory difference.

Beginning with extended boundary critique, the dotted circle represents the boundary of both the system in question and the duration of the present moment. The notion of boundary critique is extended from the boundary of system space to include time span, but more than that, the span of all six dimensions of the present moment. The line is dotted to symbolise that the present moment system boundary is permeable to influences from a greater present moment within which it is contained and also subject to the judgement of the reflexive agent or subject at the heart of the system. So the concept of present moment contributes to framing the definition of the APM.

The phenomenological aspect of the APM is the experience of duration (a) which depends on the attention (e) and cognition (f) of the reflexive subject. Duration is the experience of the present as having more to it than simply the knife-edge instant between the past and the future. Attention (e) is the capacity to direct and sustain interest in the present event.[26] Cognition (f) is the capacity to configure and interpret the experience.

An important consideration here is the attention span of the subject. Husserl (Gell, 1992) seconds differentiated the direct experience of hearing a sound as retention distinct from memory and protention as distinct from imagination. The APM extends this to the range of factors in both past and future that the subject can sustain. In conventional terms, this can be related to time-span capacity (Goodman, 1966). In the context of systemic intervention, this span relates to the intended scope of improvement, which in conventional terms is characterised as short, medium or long term. Perception (b) is the engagement in the experience by a conscious self. Retention (c) is the presence in experience of temporally recent aspects of the currently ongoing event; note this is not the same as the reproduction of the experience in memory. Protention (d) is the counterpart to retention in the experience of anticipation of the currently ongoing event; note this is not the same as the imagination of a future.

Research into time and brain structure sheds some light on this at the neurobiological level, but the field is still unresolved. The APM implies that the time experience can range beyond the short intervals of neural impulses. The situation is summarised by Damasio:

> Mind time has to do with how we experience the passage of time and how we organise chronology. Despite the steady tick of the clock, duration can seem fast or slow, short or long. And this variability can happen on different scales, from decades, seasons, weeks and hours, down to the tiniest intervals of music – the span of a note or the moment of silence between two notes. We also place events in time, deciding when they occurred, in which order and on what scale, whether that of a lifetime or of a few seconds.[27]

In the structure of APM, the first cybernetic dynamic is the adaption to feedback (g), which is the learning cycle of adaptation. This, in itself, is not anticipation but is essential for a viable system. Adaptive feedback is the capacity of the experiencing conscious self to take heed of and adjust behaviour to what has recently occurred within their present moment.

The APM structure includes the capacity to learn from past experience. This can be seen as information, as coming from the retention side of duration, which in conventional terms is characterised as adaptation, learning from history. The APM also includes the capacity to receive information from the protention side of the present moment, learning from the future. This information contains elements which cannot be derived from the past. In some current thinking about the prospective capacities of mind and brain (see, for example, Seligman et al., 2013) this is beginning to be acknowledged.

As an anticipatory system, able to incorporate both past and future into current choice, the APM exercises the intelligent flexibility of induction and reperception as distinct from deduction. Deduction favours the momentum side of the APM, whereas induction is critical, through toleration and processing of anomaly, to the open future. This capacity enables the repatterning described later in Chapter 6. Any reflexive mind has a repertoire or inventory of schema or mental models that inform behaviour at different levels. Schema inventory is the repertoire of cognitive interpretations that are available to the conscious self. The term schema refers to some organised pattern of thought or mental model that organises categories of information and the relationships amongst them. The term was given prominence by Piaget and taken up by von Glasersfeld[28] in his radical constructivism. The role of schema in sense making also features in Weik's theory.[29] Schema should not be understood as equivalent to blueprints within the mind that are in some way implemented. The situation is far more dynamic and plastic than that; cognition is neither wholly schematic nor wholly interactive, but some hybrid of the two. The plasticity of the brain seems to be constantly active with its inventory of schema as well as enacting, through the equivalent of simulation, much wider possibilities than those currently manifest. In the APM diagram this is represented by the relationship between the schema inventory (h) and the privileged schema (i) in action at any particular moment, selected as appropriate.

In behaviour which is principally adaptive, the privileged schema will be part of an existing historical repertoire which may well be applied in a novel way, but is essentially based on past experience. In behaviour which is anticipatory, the privileged schema may emerge from a shock factor which has invalidated the current repertoire as ill-fitting and inappropriate. Privileged schema are the automatically or consciously selected schema that are dominant in the current interpretation. We can suppose from this model that any authentic anticipatory behaviour is always arising from some anomaly that challenges the habitual way of responding to situations or taking decisions that have strong implications for the future. These anomalies may come in several forms. An example is when, in a scenario planning exercise, the reflexive decision-maker sees propositions in a scenario that contradict his or her current strategic assumptions and therefore indicate possible future failure if not taken into account. If these scenario propositions are taken seriously enough, a crisis of reperception is triggered. This is a non-trivial event since it almost certainly will also trigger psychological factors like denial and defensive routines (Argyris & Schon, 1978) as well as entry into new opportunity space.

However, there can be internalised forms of anticipatory reperception that emerge from a more intuitive source that transgresses patterns of conditioning. This can be observed externally in fields from competitive sport to entrepreneurial enterprise. A player in a ballgame may have an uncanny capacity to be ahead of the game in just the right spot to make winning moves. An entrepreneur may have a hunch that something unbelievable will work against all conventional wisdom, risking with confidence, seizing an opportunity overlooked or dismissed by others.

So in terms of the APM diagram pathway cognition (f)→(k) represents the mainstream of choosing how to look at the situation. The roles of the pathways are highlighted in the following three perspectives in Figure 4.6.

In summary, the APM reframes the anticipatory system as a second-order cybernetic system and sets the scene for new research in the discipline of anticipation related to decision-making, policy and governance, which all include the observer/actor/decider. The APM framework provides a heuristic for exploring different forms of conscious participation especially relevant to the human domain of practical affairs. His is an essential system enabling re-patterning. These explorations include recognizing the

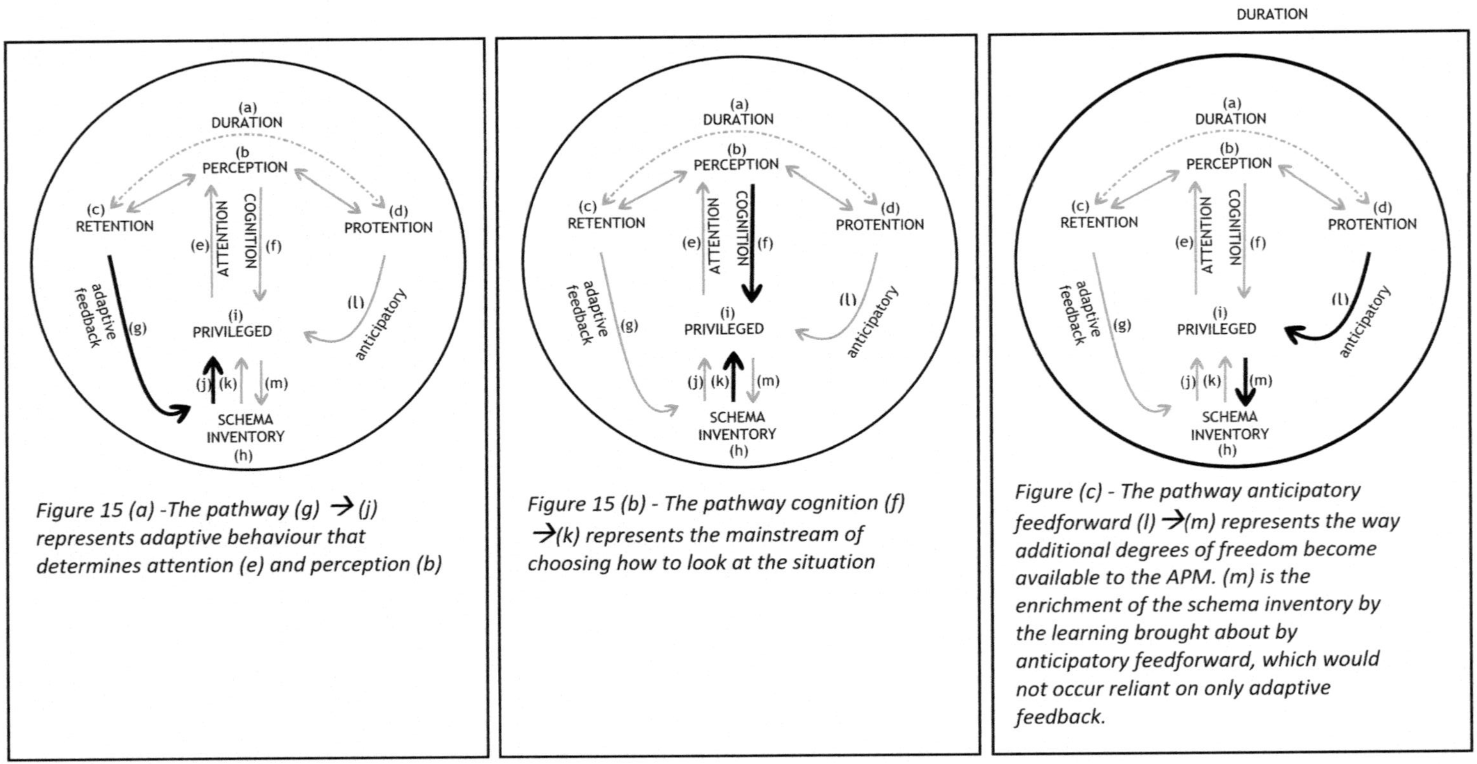

DURATION

Figure (c) - The pathway anticipatory feedforward (l) →(m) represents the way additional degrees of freedom become available to the APM. (m) is the enrichment of the schema inventory by the learning brought about by anticipatory feedforward, which would not occur reliant on only adaptive feedback.

Figure 15 (b) - The pathway cognition (f) →(k) represents the mainstream of choosing how to look at the situation

Figure 15 (a) - The pathway (g) → (j) represents adaptive behaviour that determines attention (e) and perception (b)

Figure 4.6 The three main pathways of the APM

importance of creativity in anticipatory decision-making and governance, the role of the state of mind of the decision-maker in anticipation (for example in forms of mindfulness) and the need to stimulate reperception if the confirmation biases of entrenched belief systems are to be loosened up to better embrace the presented complexity and uncertainty of the world.

So in my search the APM is a concept that helps me bring the world of conventional evidence-based 'best practice' in intimate connection with the world of disruptive innovation and creativity, including anticipation of radical futures. This provides a foundation for approach the way we go about decision-making in the hyperturbulent environment that is emerging rapidly in the Anthropocene. However, even though the concept might hang together, the practical reality is that the external turbulence is accompanied by the inner turbulence of many factors incompatible with our dominant belief systems, our habits of thinking and feeling. The 'ox' may be caught but it surely needs taming! This will be the topic of the next chapter which develops a richer understanding of what integrity in decision-making requires and how it differs from conventional analysis.

Notes

1 Arthur Young, inventor of the first commercial helicopter made the point that a mechanism comes into existence through purpose. See www.arthuryoung.com/maker1.html

2 Seligman, M. E. P., Railton, P., Baumeister, R. F., & Sripada, C. (2013). Navigating into the future or driven by the past. *Perspectives on Psychological Science, 8*, 119–141.

3 Beer, S. (1994). *Beyond dispute: The invention of team syntegrity.* Chichester: Wiley.

4 Rosen, R. (1985). *Anticipatory systems: Philosophical, mathematical and methodological foundations.* New York: Pergamon Press. Poli, R. (2010). The many aspects of anticipation. *Foresight, 12*(3), 7–17.

5 Fuerth, L. S., & Faber, E. M. H. (2012). *Anticipatory governance – practical upgrades : Equipping the executive branch to cope with increasing speed and complexity of major challenges.* Washington DC: Elliott School of International Affairs. Retrieved from http://forwardengagement.org/?option–com_content&view=article&id=6&Itemid=6

6 Poli, R. (Ed.). (2018). *Handbook of anticipation.* New York: Springer.

7 Louie, A. H. (2010). Robert Rosen's anticipatory system. *Foresight, 12*(3), 18–29.

8 Conant, R., & Ashby, R. (1970). Every good regulator of a system must be a model of that system. *International Journal of Systems Sciences, 1*(2).

9 Louie, Robert Rosen's anticipatory system.

10 von Foerster, H. (1995). Ethics and second order cybernetics. *Stanford Humanities Review, 4*(2), 308–319; Scott, B. (2004). Scott 2nd order cybernetics: An historical introduction. *Kybernetes, 33*(9/10), 1365–1378.

11 Muller, K. H. (2016). *Second-Order Science: The Revolution of Scientific Structures.* Wien: Edition Echoraum.

12 Hodgson, A. (2016). *Time, pattern, perception: Integrating systems and futures thinking* (PhD thesis). University of Hull. Retrieved from www.academia.edu

13 Rosen, *Anticipatory systems.*

14 'The idea of anticipation in science is controversial, because of "objective causality" pronounced in the "Zeroth Commandment": Thou shalt not allow future state to affect present change of state. Anticipation is almost always excluded from study at every level of system theory. The reasons for this rest on certain basic methodological presuppositions which have underlain "science" in the past few centuries: the essential basis on which "genuine scientific inquiry" rests is the principle of causality (which an anticipatory systems apparently violates); and "true objective science" cannot be argued from final cause whereas an anticipatory system seems to embody a form of teleology' (Louie, Robert Rosen's anticipatory system, p. 20).

15 Kineman, J. J., & Poli, R. (2014). Ecological literacy leadership. *Bulletin of the Ecological Society of America, 95*(1), 30–58.

16 Louie, *Robert Rosen's anticipatory system.*

17 Smolin, L. (2013). *Time reborn: From the crisis in physics to the future of the universe.* New York: Houghton Mifflin Harcourt.

18 Hodgson, A. (2013). Towards an ontology of the present moment. *On the Horizon, 21*(1), 24–38.

19 Poli, R. (2011). Steps Toward an Explicit Ontology of the Future. *Journal of Future Studies, 16,* 67–78.

20 Gell, A. (1992). *The anthropology of time: Cultural constructions of temporal maps and images.* Oxford: Berg.

21 Hodgson, Towards an ontology of the present moment, 24–38.

22 Bohm, D. (1980). *Wholeness and the implicate order.* London: Routledge and Kegan Paul. Ferret, J. (2010). Anticipatory systems in physics. *Foresight, 12*(3), 30–37.

23 Holland, J. H., Holyoak, K. J., Nisbett, R. E., & Thagard, P. R. (1986). *Induction: Processes of inference, learning and discovery.* Cambridge, MA: MIT Press,.

24 Toffler, A. (1970). *Future shock.* New York: Random House.

25 Burt, G. (2010). Revisiting and extending our understanding of Pierre Wack's the gentle art of re-perceiving. *Technological Forecasting & Social Change, 77,* 1476–1484.

26 Ingold, T. (1999). From the transmission of representations to the education of attention. In *The Debated Mind: Evolutionary Psychology versus Ethnography*, edited by H. Whitehouse, 113–53. Oxford: Berg.

27 Damasio, A. (2014). Remembering when. *Scientific American, 23*(Autumn), 42–47.

28 von Glasersfeld, E. (2001). The radical constructivist view of science. *Foundations of Science, 6*(1–3), 31–43.

29 Weber, K., & Glynn, M. A. (2006). Making sense with intuitions: Context thought and action in Karl Weik's theory. *Organization Studies, 27*(11), 163901660.

Chapter 5

Cultivating decision integrity

Step 5 – Taming the ox

> *The relating of the turbulent world to the equilibrium of the mind is a developmental task. The taming process is the internalisation and practice of a new paradigm.*

The runaway situation needs to be caught and brought into line with the more inclusive reality of subject-object integration.

So far we have made steps to reframe the paradigm of systems science to include the observer, to move our conceptions of time out of the linear time trap and indicate the importance and relevance of anticipatory systems in a second-order context. However, the aim of this reframing is to prepare the ground for changing the way we can respond to the challenge of hyperturbulence. This brings us to re-examining the nature and practice of decision-making.

Adopting a more open dimensionality with more degrees of freedom places decision-making in a different context. The external criteria of making choices becomes inseparable from the state of mind of the decision-maker. The implication is that this privileges *integrity*. Integrity is an interesting word for a world-view that acknowledges the observer because it can imply both integrity of an external system but also the internal *ethical position* of the observer. In a world where much attention has been placed on developing objective decision sciences, it may initially sound odd to attribute ethical responsibility to a 'detached' decision-maker using analytical criteria, but from a second-order perspective non-intervention is also itself an intervention. Any observer is also an actor whether active or passive. The ethics are inescapable.

Even the most 'objective' decisions are shaped and coloured by the decision-maker's world-view, which by its very nature carries unconscious assumptions with it. Systems thinking, taken largely as a first-order discipline, is not free from this limitation. However, I believe its practitioners could do a better job of becoming conscious of this limitation. This is evidenced by some practitioners growing more interested in the notions of second-order cybernetics and second-order science. From this perspective the Cartesian/Newtonian split appears, paradoxically, as a special second-order position in which its practitioners have agreed deliberately or tacitly to eliminate themselves as observers and then buried that they have done this! But as Maturana pointed out, every observation is carried out by an observer. This forms a basis for a new understanding of decision integrity from which we can change the practices of decision-making to be better able to cope with hyperturbulence.

This is the fifth stage of ox herding.

~~~~~

The trap of rationality

The adoption and of rise management sciences as the primary 'paradigm' in commerce and public affairs, and taught widely in business schools, originated in a period when rational decision-making was considered the solution to complicated situations. Since then there has been a largely unexamined fixation with rational decision-making, although real decisions are often made by vested interests, heedless of any analysis. Rational economic man has become the unit in modern management, and mathematical decision analysis has become the dominant espoused basis of management. Yet this legacy approach is increasingly incongruent with the turbulent world in which we find ourselves.

This rational decision mind-set belongs to the high agency / low uncertainty domain of Figure 3.2 in Chapter 3. The *implicit* view in the rational approach to the operating environment is something like 'this is what we want; this is what is going to happen in the world; so we know what we are going to do in that world in order to get what we want'. Herein lies the trap. The world is continuously changing, it is complex and it throws out events and properties which are outside any range of prediction. Such events have been characterised as the phenomena of 'black swans'.[1] The black swan theory refers to the implications of large-impact, hard-to-predict and rare events beyond the realm of normal expectations. In the hyperturbulent world, black swans come thicker and faster, no longer an exception but inclining to be the norm.

We are part of this world, not separate from it, so we are of the same nature. When we rationalise ourselves and our world we are asserting something which at best is of limited consistency with how things really are seen, for example, by complexity science. The perverse consequence of this is that the more we assert this form of our understanding of the world, the more we find ourselves living with the unintended consequences of our decisions. Turbulence morphs into hyperturbulence.

This view can be applied to the individual, the group, the institution, the nation and the globe. From a management perspective we focus on the institution or organisation. Organisation management, dominated by the management sciences, has analysed and systematised situations to bring them under control to pursue goals such as 'return to shareholders' or 'public value'. But as the global contextual crisis looms ever more strongly, such limited and limiting goals, often disguising more nefarious aims associated with power and greed rather than sustainability and strategic adaptation, are dissociated from the real world.

However, the real world leaks out from the boundaries of rationality, springs surprises on us and confronts us with uncertainties. Indeed, on occasion, the world smashes through the very centre of institutional life and destroys jobs, companies, industries and even whole economies. The situation this places civilisation in is as an impending casualty. Rational control should be seen for what it is, a convenient half-truth, where the other half of the truth has caught up with us.

The kind of decision-making that dominates in the 'controlled world' does not match the behaviour of the 'uncontrollable world'. Effective decisions cannot be arrived at by rational analysis alone, because the rationale is inherently a limited perspective. We need the half-truth this generates, but we need an approach to deal with the missing unruly half.

Some thinkers and practitioners have made efforts to create alternative modes of perception, analysis and decision-making more congruent with this unruly world beyond the veneer of socio-economic rationality. The International Futures Forum[2] sums up its foundational work in addressing these issues in a text, *Ten Things to Do in a Conceptual Emergency*. This puts forward ten strategic principles that offer prospects for working towards the other half of truth not accessible to rational analysis. The following subset of five of their principles, summarised here, helps to frame this approach to decision integrity.

> *Give up on the myth of control*
> We have taken our ever more sophisticated models as a proxy for reality. But our models break down in the face of the real complexity and mystery of the world.

> *Trust subjective experience*
> The implications for how we see the world and our place in it are critical for our understanding of it and our behaviour towards it and, more profoundly, as part of it.

> *Form and nurture integrities*
> The traditional model of organisation is struggling. Start by replacing integration with the more flexible and adaptable notion of integrity.

> *Reperceive the present*
> We underestimate the importance of living more deeply and consciously in the present. We need to extend our habits of what counts as 'knowledge'.

> *Move beyond an enlightenment consciousness*
> The subject-object split is the hallmark of the Enlightenment, the separation of self from the world. We need to recognise a new context.

A distinction can be made between a decision field and a decision process. The decision field is the context of decision, its environment and all the external factors that will have some bearing on the decision. The field is in the present but also has attached to it histories giving it momentum and futures in the sense of trends and emerging patterns. The decision process is how the human decision-maker conducts himself or herself to investigate, assess and intervene in the decision field. Aspects of the decision process are unconscious, like habits of mind and a taken-for-grantedness of the nature of the decision field. Other aspects are designed according to disciplines and understandings and could be called the decision system. The decision system can also be viewed as the espoused theory (Argyris, 1990) of the decision-makers.

Clearly, for successful outcomes, there needs to be sufficient correspondence between the decision process and the decision field, the latter usually being largely outside the control of the decision-makers. For example, a market may be moving in a certain way which will prescribe the range of options for choice. In an expanding market the choices may be about investment in growth opportunities; in a shrinking market the choices may be about competitive strengthening or about exit strategies.

When the world is behaving in a reasonably predicable and forecastable way (the left side of Figure 3.2), the decision process can be based on technical analysis, such as net present value or cost/benefit, and the outcomes will tend to be as hoped for. Indeed, accumulated successes in this way will become ingrained in the generic type of decision process as the success formula for that world.

If the world is actually more complex, more interconnected and more uncertain (the right side of Figure 3.2) than presumed, there is a mismatch between the decision process and the decision field. To be successful the appreciation of the decision field must keep up with changing circumstances. The decision system has to take into account an unruly rather than a predictable world.

So there are two obstacles to anticipatory decision-making in the face of complexity and uncertainty. In the business as usual decision process, however intelligently and thoroughly carried out, the mental model of the decision-maker is not treated as part of the system in question (Hodgson, 2010).[3] It stands outside it in the 'observer distinct from the observed' mode. It is first order – 'It is the principle of objectivity that the properties of the observer shall not enter into the description of his observation' (von Foerster, 1995, p. 3).

Decision as learning

Although multiple structural anticipatory scenarios (Sharpe & van der Heijden, 2007) can help create mental conditions for revealing the hazards, they cannot deal with the framing of decisions in their context. The usual result is that decision-makers, having engaged with the decision field as a set of scenarios, reach for the familiar tools of decision analysis and project the rational onto the unruly. In reaching for rules to give them the answer (say, passing a hurdle rate) they collapse any benefits of the scenario structure. The fundamental incongruence between the complex uncertain nature of the decision field and the assumption-limited algorithms of the decision process has then been retained. Some attempts to overcome this introduce systems thinking into the decision process. For example, system dynamics simulations of different scenarios through micro-worlds can create a game-like engagement with them and help engage the decision-maker into a different frame of reference, one that has feedback on the consequences of the decision-maker's choices compared to the usual one.[4] This approach was clearly recognised as a step forward by Arie de Geus[5] in his discussion of the nature of play in learning and the different process that is needed to switch from assimilative learning to accommodative learning as defined by Piaget. The treatment of decision-making as a subjective learning process as well as an objective analytical process points to a whole new approach to decision-making under uncertainty.

De Geus makes the point that

> the real decision-making process is a learning process rather than the application of knowledge. Many at high levels of management are convinced they are there because of what they know and how they represent what they are. These statements were saying you're not there because of what you know. You're there because you're reasonably good at intuitively or otherwise finding your way to a learning process together with your colleagues, such that you learn and arrive at new conclusions that are more or less successful.[6]

The need for decision as learning is strengthened by considering the decision system in the context of cybernetics. Particularly relevant is the role of Ashby's law of requisite variety[7] in a guidance system. Let us suppose that the decision system has a primary goal. It might be to make money, to heal the sick or to win a team game. The decision field has a quasi-infinite set of states or variables, only some of which can be known and predicted. We have established the mismatch between the decision process and the decision field. Ashby's Law states in effect that the greater the variety of the context, the greater the need for variety in the guidance system. Stafford Beer summarised this as variety absorbs variety. This implies that the higher the variety (complexity) of the decision system, the larger the range of perturbations that can be accommodated or compensated. It leads to the somewhat counterintuitive observation that the decision system (individual or group) must have a sufficiently large variety of options in order to ensure a sufficiently small variety of outcomes in achieving the goal. This principle has important implications for hyperturbulent situations: since the variety of perturbations in such a context is potentially unlimited, we should always try to increase its internal variety (or diversity) so as to be optimally prepared for any foreseeable or unforeseeable contingency; hence the importance of learning.

This challenge of linking the reframed decision field to the actual mental frame of the decision-maker was clear to Pierre Wack, a key originator of scenario thinking. In making his final critique to Shell executives and planners of the state of strategic planning and especially the use of scenarios, he strongly affirmed the point that unless the decision-maker himself or herself actually changes in the process of arriving at a choice, the exercise is useless. He names this 'the gentle art of reperception'. For Wack[8] the shift in perception of the decision-makers was an essential component of the decision system if scenario planning is to be successful. The decision-maker needed to enact his or her intentions as a mental rehearsal in the context of the scenarios. To explore this further we need to consider how the interaction between decider and decision field can lead to shifts in the nature of strategies and decisions.

What is a decision emerging from reperception? We must first distinguish between those kinds of decisions which are delegable to constructed systems (such as computer algorithms) and those requiring the specific insight of human beings. In an age where more and more decisions are delegated to artificial intelligence systems (some of which can often perform better than most human beings at some tasks), why are humans other than a temporary expedient only needed until all significant decisions can be delegated to artificial intelligence? The necessity for the human being in decision-making arises where there is a need for integrity.[9] Integrity has several aspects to it. It implies integration in the sense of taking into account a whole picture, in which the decision is framed in a wider context than that of the immediate concern – for example regarding the long-term implications, not just the short-term payoff. Also taken into account is the spatial and structural context of interconnections, linkages and feedbacks. So integrity implies taking into account the *big when* and the *big where* as a greatly expanded present moment.

Integrity also involves an ethical dimension, a sensitivity to values, and a degree of consistency in relation to those values that transcend the optimising and satisficing nature[10] of the situation in question. In a complex world these two sides of integrity, the holistic and the ethical, often are in seeming contradiction. In a system where economics is dominant, the ethical is considered secondary and even itself 'unethical' by viewpoints such as the Chicago school, who assert there is only one social responsibility of business – to use its resources to engage only in activities designed to increase its profits and shareholder monetary value.

Another approach to decision-making under uncertainty is that of risk mitigation. When faced with a set of uncertainties which cover a range of future states, some of which are unfavourable, the uncertainties constitute a hazard. When we form an intent to act within that hazardous situation we are faced with a risk. The manner in which we deal with that risk will challenge us with an ethical dilemma. In a situation where the risk frame is more complex than a simple good/bad choice and the ethical frame is more complex than a simple right/wrong choice, we are faced with a need for decision integrity. This is especially so when emergent circumstances present us with incalculable issues and *destroy the rule book's validity*.

This discussion so far might lead us to believe that as long as we can learn enough we can decide. But this restricts learning to evidence from the past. Given the gap between the high variety of the decision field and the restricted variety of the decision system, there are increasing numbers of questions which are not decidable by rules and assumptions. In the first-order mode, however intelligently and thoroughly carried out, the mental model of the decision-maker is not treated as part of the system in question. It stands outside of it in the 'observer distinct from the observed' mode. It is first order.

Von Foerster points out[11] that it took some time in the early days of cybernetics for the idea to catch on that there is a limitation to the classical scientific paradigm, in which the observer is separated from the observed. The implication in management science is that the properties of the decision-maker shall not enter the analysis of the decision space. Breaking out of this paradigm to the view that the observer has to give account of him or herself in the system in question creates a whole new perspective. He points out that 'this perception represents a fundamental change not only in the way we conduct science, but also how we perceive of teaching, of learning, of the therapeutic process, of organisational management, and so on and so forth' (p. 4).

Now von Foerster goes on to make a profound but simple observation that relates back to the introductory remarks about decision integrity. In the first-order paradigm, decision analysis is considered independent of the analyst and can be informed by the rules of analysis as to what the 'optimum' decision is. Any quantitative judgement is based on an explicit or implicit moral code. By contrast, in the second-order paradigm, the decision-maker is considered part of the system under decision and can only tell himself or herself what the 'best' decision is. This, von Foerster points out, is the origin of ethics and that ethics cannot be articulated as a code. The rewards of ethical action lie in the action itself.

In the paradigm where the decision-maker is independent of the decision field, as in the mode of classical science, the aim of decision-framing and analysis is to render the initial question decidable. Von Foerster also points out that as well as this type of question there are other kinds of question that are in principle *undecidable*. Whether we recognise such questions and how we treat them if we do is the crux of the matter.

The notion of undecidable questions

We need to consider the mental model of the decision-maker and indeed for him or her to consider reflectively their own mental model. Clemson's[12] treatment of management cybernetics is helpful in representing the basis of this issue. In his discussion of the operational unit in the context of Beer's viable systems model (VSM), he describes a set of relationships as shown in Figure 5.1.

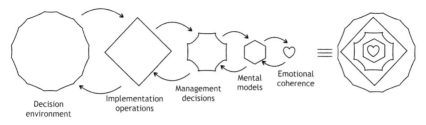

Figure 5.1 An operational unit in viable systems and the
nested nature of the levels

Modified for decision-making, the decision environment is the contextual
field in which the decision is taken. This is also the high variety, unpredictable and unruly world upon which we impose our scientific or rational order.
Within that environment and of considerably less variety is the implementation operation, which is the vehicle of the decision. It could be an organisation or a project. It has a reciprocal relationship with the environment, acting
upon it and being acted upon. This, in turn, is subject to a management decision that is an intervention by the decision-maker. He or she is steering the
ship, so to speak, also with a two-way interaction based on a mental model.
Interventions are of even less variety than the operations themselves and the
feedback from the operations is highly filtered information. The variety of
the decision system is less than that of the decided-upon operation. The decision-maker's approach to the steering action is therefore framed by the mental model of the decision-maker, represented in Figure 16a as the hexagon. In
other words, how they view the world is a determinant of the interventions
made. This is also a two-way relationship which may be static or dynamic.
In the static mode, equivalent to Argyris's single-loop learning,[13] the main
interaction between the mental model and the management intervention is
error correction. In the dynamic mode, equivalent of Argyris's double-loop
learning the interaction is assumption revision, implying an enrichment of
the mental model. If this second-order learning does not take place, there is a
gap between 'espoused theory' and 'theory in use'. At either level the mental
model is being enacted in its engagement with the decision field.

The mental model of the decision-maker may be more or less sophisticated. It may be very complex but still linear. It may be informed by systems
thinking and cybernetics and enriched with dynamic loops. In this case we
could say that the decision system of manager/operation/environment is
working in a frame of first-order cybernetics. This offers some movement
towards decision integrity in a complex, interconnected world.

In a second-order perspective the different components in Figure 5.1 are
actually embedded in each other. In other words the emotional tone, represented by the heart in the diagram, is embedded in the mental model, the

decision-maker, the operation and the environment, as shown in Figure 1b. Thus we can see that the decider is actually part of the decision environment or decision field. The decision-maker then is exercising a cognitive system which is not distinct from his or her history of action in the decision field. This perspective has much in common with the view that cognition is enactive. In this view representation is taken to be separated from action, whether the realism of construction of a mental model from external information or the idealism as the projection of a pregiven inner world. Varela, Thompson and Rosch consider the real situation to be a 'middle way' between these two opposites.[14] They state that we can

> situate cognition as embodied action within the context of evolution as natural drift provides a view of cognitive capacities as inextricably linked histories that are *lived*, much like paths that exist only as they are laid down in walking. Consequently cognition is no longer seen as problem solving on the basis of representations; instead cognition in its most encompassing sense consists of the enactment or bringing forth of a world by a viable history of structural coupling.

From this perspective we acknowledge that the whole of the cybernetic structure is itself enclosed in a meta mental model which might be considered as the world-view of the decider.

From the perspective of both second-order cybernetics and enactive cognition, the separation of decider from decision field is a misleading construct. They are inseparably bound together and the pathway taken by the decider is reciprocally bound up with the decision field and the outcome of any decision.

The implications that the decision system includes the decider is an issue of consciousness and its relationship to the properties of systems. Consciousness comes into consideration because we are now affirming learning as a function of the human decider and because there is an ethical dimension to choice. The properties of systems enters our considerations because, in a holistic decision system there is feedback or reflexivity. Reperception implies a change of consciousness and choice implies taking responsibility for the consequences of decisions.

For example, the reflexive world-view leads to seemingly paradoxical assertions like the following, which nevertheless show up in critical decision situations:

A implies B, B implies C, C implies A

or

A implies B, B implies A

or

A implies A

What is the nature of decision-making and the ethical responsibility of the decider in the context of a turbulent world? Von Foerster (1995) makes the point that only decisions about undecidable questions carry the quality of ethical responsibility. Where a question is decidable through rational analysis or 'mathematical economics', there is no real decision and the best we can hope for is some kind of application of a moral rule behind which the decision-maker takes shelter. Faced with an undecidable question there is nowhere to shelter. In this latter case, responsibility must reside in the decision-maker's action or choice itself. Von Foerster explains why the only *undecidable* questions demand *real* decisions:

> Simply because the decidable questions are already decided by the choice of the framework in which they are asked, and by the choice of rules of how to connect what we call "the question" with what we may take for an "answer". In some cases it may go fast, in others it may take a long, long time, but ultimately we will arrive, after a sequence of compelling logical steps, at an irrefutable answer: a definite Yes, or a definite No.[15]

If we separate the decider from the decision field, decision rules can be applied to the field and, if sufficiently ingenious, the question and automatic selection of an answer is rendered decidable. But as von Foerster points out, selecting is not true choosing. 'Only those questions that are in principle undecidable, we can decide'. And this is the condition of navigating in the face of turbulence. So there is a close relationship between ethics and choice in the rapid responses and anticipations needed in the face of turbulence.

The implication here is that a state of mind or consciousness of the decider is critical for high adaptive performance. If the decider changes state, the decision field changes state; therefore, both the practical options and their ethical implications come into the foreground. The induction theory helps us to understand that there is a different operation of the cognitive system needed to deal with undecidable questions. But the cognitive system must also be recognised as a re-entrant system. The implications of this are summarised by von Foerster like this:

> we are under no compulsion, not even under that of logic, when we decide upon in principle undecidable questions. There is no external necessity that forces us to answer such questions one way or another. We are free! The complement to necessity is not chance, it is choice! We can choose who we wish to become when we have decided on in principle undecidable questions.[16]

The navigational implications of second-order decision

So far we have concentrated on the second-order system. But decisions are also taking place in contexts of multiple human beings in organisations. The system in question then becomes more complex. With regard to an organisation of human beings is it possible for there to be genuine decisions about undecidable questions? Generally our institutions are invented to avoid ethically responsible decisions and place them in a context of rules and frameworks in which everyone either is 'told to do it' or 'had no choice'.

The undecidable question, because of its inherent uncertainty, requires an ethical commitment that cannot be arrived at by applying business-as-usual rules whether they be financial or moral. This also means that the decision-maker's current mental model, which is often a fixed hierarchical structure of categories and sub-categories, is an inadequate basis for rapid adaptive decisions.

Van der Heijden recognises over many years of observation and participation in high-level strategy work that decisions are arrived at by a reflexive decision process which is essentially one of mutual learning.

> The learning loop model shows the interwovenness of thinking and action. If action is based on planning on the basis of a mental model, then institutional action must be based on a shared mental model. Only through a process of conversation can elements of personal observation and thought be structured and embedded in the accepted and shared organisational theories-in-use. Similarly new perceptions of opportunities and threats, based on the reflection on experiences of actions playing out in the environment, can only become institutional property through conversation.[17]

However, the reflexive mutual accommodation of strategic conversation is still a rarity in management. Management cultures are dominated by non-negotiable hierarchy and by the domination of powerful individuals who may seek advice but are not open to reflexive review of their biases and beliefs. The result is an absence of learning, a tendency to repeat previous mistakes, large-scale external diseconomies and an absence of ethical decision-making.

Managers practising decision integrity will reflect on their role more on the following lines, consistent with a second-order viewpoint.

> The recognition that I, the decision-maker, am faced with undecidable questions that are nevertheless unavoidable;

That this places me within, not outside, the system in which I am a manager and hence in the reflexive context;

That I am inescapably faced with ethical dilemmas that cannot be reduced to moral rules. I must therefore make free choices and take responsibility;

That any choice amongst options made are a function of my own state of mind and understanding in conjunction with my colleagues;

That the nature of being in an organisation with mutual responsibility with others means that the essence of shaping a decision is dialogic and emergent as distinct from analytic and persuasive;

That if my exploration of the nature of the decision field and its context (stimulated, for example, by a well-crafted scenario set) does not alter my perceptions, I have not properly engaged with the decision task (the reperception issue). If the possible future worlds do not change me then I am still in the detached observer paradigm and failing in responsibility.

The act of reperception is the antithesis of a copying machine. It is an act of induction, of learning. The support that framework-based decision-making becomes a weakness in the face of undecidable questions. This weakness arises from ingrained subconscious mental patterns that are difficult to change. We think we are peering into the windscreen of the future but are actually fixated on the view in the rear-view mirror. It usually takes the shock consequences of a bend in the road to realise that we have ceased learning. The point here is that our decision-making needs to be, as well as consistent with the six points, a learning process.

Von Foerster summarises the position this way: 'With the essence of observing, namely the processes of cognition, being removed, the observer is reduced to a copying machine, and the notion of responsibility has been successfully juggled away'.[18]

There is an inherent psychological and cultural resistance to the proposition that real ethical decisions inevitably change the decision-maker who cannot be abstracted from the decision system. In today's world of applied management science in fields such as financial management, the mathematisation of making money inevitably leads to breakdown both systemically and ethically. There are no 'masters of the universe' because, in reality, the fallible human being has not actually been removed from the decision system. The abdication of responsibility to 'copying machines' has its unavoidable consequences. The factors which colour ethics and responsibility are buried in propaganda and kept there by greed and attachment to power. But in actual fact the decision-maker is never outside of the decision system.

One of the characteristics of hyperturbulence is that is presents us with a stream of undecidable questions and therefore the presence of the decision-maker is required to keep affirming ethical choices.

Implications for management and governance

One conclusion from this exploration is that we have a legacy of applied management science that is incongruent with the increasingly unruly nature of the real world. Further, by carrying on with mismatching decision processes we are actually exacerbating the situation. In the new global era, continuing the objectification of the world assumes that we are not part of the world system, obscuring the reflexivity of our actions in the quest for control, certainty and predictability. Just as Newtonian science finds itself subsumed in a larger paradigm of relativity and quantum physics, so observer detached management science will find itself subsumed in a larger and more reflexive notion of that science. Discussion of this is beyond the scope of a single chapter but it is important to recognise that management science is not actually detached from the current transition to the global age. Albrow[19] puts this in context by making the case that the era of modernity, which is deeply enmeshed in the objectivist science paradigm has come to the end of the road. The new situation is globality which confronts us with bigger and potentially more fatal issues of responsibility for limits and consequences of our decisions.

Decision integrity, as a management capability can only be developed by its practice. It requires the courage to take decisions and ethical responsibility in the face of consciously recognised undecidable uncertainties. Where things are predictable and decision analysis is used there is no real choice in the sense of discriminative cognition because the answer falls out of the rules, not from a reflective human choice. Some differences between first-order and second-order decision-making are summarised in the Table 5.1.

The implications of this analysis are that, from the perspective of second-order cybernetics, most decisions are not decisions at all but selections derived from systems which logically or computationally provide a 'decidable' answer for a passive observer. Since the passivity of the observer is nevertheless subject to psychological biases, distortions of motivation and even deliberate corruption it is hardly surprising that we live in a society full of unintended consequences for which no one will take responsibility. There are not only consequences for decision outcomes of decision-makers but also for the whole future of organisations and society. On the other hand, we also live in a time when forms of co-operation are reconfiguring

Table 5.1 Comparison of decision-making in forecastable
and in turbulent situations

DECISIONS IN FORECASTABLE SITUATIONS	DECISIONS IN TURBULENT SITUATIONS
• Susceptible to decision analysis • Can be modelled with first-order cybernetics or systems theory • Abdicates responsibility to 'the system' or decision rules • Values are 'mechanised' as impersonal moral (or immoral) rules and conditions • Consequences subsumed into the predictive tools and techniques • Skills of decision *analysis* predetermined or configured to give a calculable outcome • Error and failure are attributed to changes context and external circumstances	• Decision analysis insufficient • Requires shift to second-order cybernetics • Requires decision-maker to assume ethical responsibility • Values embodied in the personal ethics of the decision-makers • Consequences continuously monitored in the act of observing the observer – reflexive • Skills of creative decision *thinking* and dialogue exercised by the decision-makers • Error and failure are treated as feedback to the decision-makers as collaborative learners

social integrities beyond the forms of institution that combine classical power hierarchy and applied management science.

In this emerging world we need to move from the idea of a certain organisation navigating through a world of uncertainty to a world in which *the enterprise itself is inherently uncertain*. Put simply, we are dealing with *uncertainty multiplied by uncertainty*! Being caught in our previous set of assumptions and world-views drives us deeper into the conceptual emergency indicated in the introduction to this chapter. The way out of the emergency is to evolve our scientific world-view to a new level of insight and complexity.

Decision integrity as concept, method and state of mind deeply enriched by the APM and its supporting principles offers a calmness in the midst of turbulence and thus the 'ox' is tamed. But what may be accomplished by the individual in their own experience and practice is still inadequate for the Anthropocene hyperturbulence. This leads us to the necessity to find ways of individuals flexibly collaborating in ways that transcend organisation institutions and their limited interests in a manner able to navigate hyperturbulence. This is the topic of the next chapter.

Notes

1 Taleb, N. N. (2007). *The black swan: The impact of the highly improbable*. New York: Random House.
2 Leicester, G., & O'Hara, M. (2009). *Ten things to do in a conceptual emergency*. Aberdour, Scotland: IFF/Triarchy.
3 Hodgson, Anthony. 'Decision Integrity and Second Order Cybernetics'. In *Cybernetics and Systems Theory in Management: Tools, Views and Advancements*, edited by Stephen Wallis, 52–74. Hershey: IGI Global, 2010.
4 Langley, P. A., & Morecroft, J. (1996). Learning from microworld environments: A summary of research issues. In G. P. Richardson & J. D. Sterman (Eds.), *System Dynamics '96*. Cambridge, MA: System Dynamics Society.
5 de Geus, A. (1997). *The living company*. London: Nichlas Brealey.
6 de Geus, loc cit.
7 Ashby, R. (1960). *Design for a brain*. London: Chapman and Hall.
8 Wack, P. (1985). Scenarios: The gentle art of re-perceiving. *Harvard Business Review*.
9 Kurtzweil, R. (1990). *The age of intelligent machines*. Cambridge, MA: MIT Press.
10 Simon, H. A. (1996). *The sciences of the artificial*. Cambridge, MA: The MIT Press.
11 von Foerster, H. (1995). Ethics and second order cybernetics. *Stanford Humanities Review, 4*(2), 308–319.
12 Clemson, B. (1984). *Cybernetics: A new management tool*. Tunbridge Wells: Abacus Press.
13 Argyris, C. (1990). *Overcoming organizational defenses – facilitating organizational learning*. Boston: Allyn and Bacon.
14 Varela, F. J., Thompson, E., & Rosch, E. (1991). *The embodied mind: cognitive science and human experience*. Cambridge, MA: The MIT Press.
15 von Foerster, Ethics and second order cybernetics.
16 von Foerster, loc cit, p. 7).
17 van der Heijden, K. (2005). *Scenarios: The art of strategic conversation* (2nd ed.). Chichester: Wiley.
18 von Foerster, Ethics and second order cybernetics, p. 7.
19 Albrow, M. (1997). *The global age*. Stanford, CA: Stanford University Press.

Chapter 6

The co-creative way

Step 6 – Riding the ox home

The observer is no longer an isolated centre but rather a node in an extended network. The individual is no longer alone but is open to intersubjective creative exploration of systems knowledge. But the music of method is also required.

The combination of complexity, emergence, chaos, uncertainty and runaway causality are beyond comprehension of the single human brain despite its amazing complexity. To navigate this emerging world we need a whole new level of collective intelligence that is able to co-create situations that correspond to the new state of affairs. And do this rapidly. There are some conditions for this to be effective.

One condition derives from the principle in cybernetics that any model held by a governor of a system needs to match the complexity of the system. This is a consequence of Ashby's law of requisite variety. In first-order terms this often is taken to be the number of states in the system in question, but from a second-order perspective it also requires requisite *qualitative* variety.

Another condition is that methods of interaction and communication need to transcend the limitation of short-term available thinking space for mentally manipulating patterns of ideas, often summarised as 7 +/– 2. Even twenty variables can have well over a million possible combinatorial patterns. So a collection of brains need a shared way of depicting as much of this complexity in as meaningful a way as possible. Shared visualisation is essential.

A further condition is that the collaborative system of people needs to be itself an anticipatory system able to operate in practice in a self-constructed APM. To operate in this system also requires a leap in emotional intelligence so that the myriad obstructive traits in the human personality do not interfere in or distort the process. Emotional coherence in the group is another essential condition.

For collective creative intelligence to operate we need to radically reform the way we meet as humans to find coherent and effective responses. The work I have done with my colleagues is to distil a core principle that is mandatory for this to work. This is *participative repatterning*. Individuals (head and heart) need to be able to repattern not only their thinking but also their deeper belief systems. This requires new levels of emotional and spiritual intelligence. This needs to take place in concert with their collaborators such that the collective becomes a super-intelligence and avoids the risk of becoming, as a collective, less intelligent than even an individual. Sadly, this collapse is all too prevalent in phenomena like 'group think' and crowd conditioning. But there are methods to counteract this and enable release of new higher-level capacity.

First, we will clarify pattern thinking and then indicate how repatterning can be carried out in the context of teamwork through participative methods.

This is the sixth stage of ox herding.

~~~~~

Pattern thinking

Given all the considerations covered in the first five chapters about the nature of the turbulence challenge, the importance of including the observer, the cultivation of future consciousness (Lombardo, 2006), the anticipatory present moment and the need for a new integrity of decision-making, it is clear that the current repertoire of systems thinking as it stands is inadequate for the task. This is not just a technical question of the principles and concepts of systems thinking but also the manner in which it is incorporated in adaptive and transformative application in society. Three fresh ingredients need to be introduced to the mix. They are variety, pattern and shared consciousness.

By variety I am referring to the principle that Ross Ashby first enunciated and Stafford Beer developed. The principle of requisite variety indicates that the effective governance of a systems requires a level of variety that matches the variety of that which is governed. Variety is usually defined as the number of possible states of the system. This is insufficient because in world where qualities are deemed significant there is the question of *requisite qualitative variety*.

By pattern I am referring to the implicit structuring of the world (even turbulence has a structure) that is apprehended through recognition of recurring patterns. Usually patterns are recognised through their embodiment in things, but in a turbulent world *things* are not where we need to be mostly paying attention. We need to attend to *processes*, to discontinuous changes and to shifts of quality as well as quantity. The way we are able to do this is through the further cultivation of a natural ability we have called *pattern thinking*.

By shared consciousness I mean the capacity for several people to generate and share a greater understanding of a situation and act coherently in the midst of it. This is hard enough in a stable situation but is even harder in a turbulent one. There are layers to shared consciousness. First, there is the manner of representation of that shared understanding, which is some form of language. However, for pattern thinking, verbal languages are limited by their syntax, so diagrammatic methods on the one hand and mathematical methods on the other hand need to be called into play. Second, there is the sharing of mental models or maps taken as our internal representations and interpretations of what is going on. Third, there is the meaning making, sense making and semantics of the players in the group. Fourthly there is the degree of shared wakefulness and mindfulness of the group which includes its ethos and guiding values. Finally, there is the skill of letting go and unlearning such that the 're' in repatterning can take place. This complex of factors we will summarise as *responsive participation*.

Pattern thinking is broader than but includes systems thinking. It is a form of cognition which contrasts with analysis. Analytical thinking is based on various logics of taking complex wholes and dividing them up into selective parts. Parts are treated separately and might be assembled together rather than synthesised back to the original whole. This approach proves very effective for many kinds of problem solving but is inappropriate in a world dominated by high rates of change occurring in complex systems with high uncertainty and emergence.

The situation today requires forms of pattern thinking that correspond better to the complexity and turbulence of the environment. Pattern thinking is a different form of cognition which evokes the synthesis power of the mind, taking it beyond solving problems to navigating turbulence. This cognitive power also differs from analytical thinking in that its effectiveness depends on a corresponding emotional intelligence and a sense of physical space and geometric symbolism. Pattern recognition, when applied to new situations requires intuitive and motivational involvement. It is about practical engagement rather than abstract analysis. Another component of pattern thinking is its relationship to change, especially radical or transformational change. In this respect it is not a static pattern but a dynamic patterning. The cognitive process is cognitive repatterning, which has a close relationship with the capacity for creative thinking.

Pattern thinking is greatly enhanced by visual thinking. Our visual capacity is our strongest way of engaging with pattern (although all our senses can be involved in some way or another, for example auditory patterns in music). Visual support can enable more powerful thinking. An analogy would be to compare playing chess with or without a chess board. There is a further step where the analogy of chess breaks down. In dynamic pattern thinking it is as if the chess board itself is a dynamic pattern which is changing with circumstances. There is another crucial role in the visual support of pattern thinking, namely its ability to facilitate shared thinking, both appreciative and creative. By having external representations of the patterns in use, different people can compare notes and more easily collaborate.

The implications of all this taken together is that there is a whole development of know-how, skill and psychological insight required to practice and facilitate this approach. To appreciate how different this know-how is from our customary ways of meeting, collaborating and attempting group understanding, some basic psychology is needed.

Dynamic thinking requires two properties of the reflexive thought process: (a) the recognition of underlying patterns of thought and (b) the movement of the constituents of thought into different juxtapositions to reveal new meanings and insights (Koestler, 1967). The key here is the capacity to sustain successive movement from one pattern to another seeking better anticipation and therefore better fit with emerging circumstances. The emphasis shifts from stasis to *kinetics*. The reconfiguring of thought patterns becomes the foreground with static patterns as a resource in the background, a figure/ground reversal. This is a metacognitive skill.[1]

Dynamic repatterning is at the heart of the anticipatory present moment (APM). There are three layers of challenge in the centre of the system in Figure 4.5. Information from the three dimensions of the past which can help learning has to be processed, and this will affect the patterning in the mind. Resistance will block learning and adaptation. What is much more difficult, information from the three dimensions of the future needs to be assimilated and may require radical repatterning. Third, a reflective intuitive judgement has to be made as to which reframing of the schema is to taken as a basis for decision and action. This is the metacognitive act of decision thinking.

The gestalt of pattern recognition

The patterning and repatterning process is the fundamental factor that is much enabled by specific forms of visual language and communication. A good starting point to explore the role of perception in configuring representational patterns before introducing conceptual frameworks, is considering the implications of the six principles of Gestalt theory and how they relate to dynamic pattern thinking.

Whereas verbal language has restricted linkage (e.g. subject-verb-object), visual language enables multiple simultaneous relationships between elements. Semantic units are potentially multi-valent. A given topology will enable some patterns of connection and exclude others hence a range of topological types is necessary. The same elements at one level can recur in different higher level topologies and linkages with different overall meanings. This is extremely difficult to codify in verbal language, where units of meaning are connected in patterns of integral meaning by grammar and syntax. In visual language integral meaning is arrived at by spatial positions and relationships. In Gestalt psychology there are six principles that codify the make-up of visual patterns.

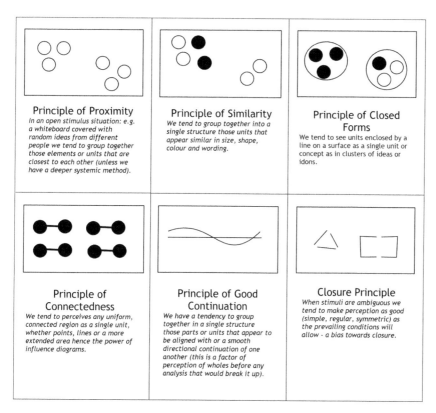

Principle of Proximity
In an open stimulus situation: e.g. a whiteboard covered with random ideas from different people we tend to group together those elements or units that are closest to each other (unless we have a deeper systemic method).

Principle of Similarity
We tend to group together into a single structure those units that appear similar in size, shape, colour and wording.

Principle of Closed Forms
We tend to see units enclosed by a line on a surface as a single unit or concept as in clusters of ideas or idons.

Principle of Connectedness
We tend to perceives any uniform, connected region as a single unit, whether points, lines or a more extended area hence the power of influence diagrams.

Principle of Good Continuation
We have a tendency to group together in a single structure those parts or units that appear to be aligned with or a smooth directional continuation of one another (this is a factor of perception of wholes before any analysis that would break it up).

Closure Principle
When stimuli are ambiguous we tend to make perception as good (simple, regular, symmetric) as the prevailing conditions will allow - a bias towards closure.

Figure 6.1 The six visual codes of gestalt

These six principles can be applied in varying ways in combination with visual topologies. Each major topology has a range of variants; for visual facilitation for group understanding any method applied needs to incorporate the most suitable topology. The most common types of topology are

- the matrix/table;
- circles – concentric or overlapping;
- free form networks – connected by lines or arrows;
- radial networks;
- closed (loop) networks;
- open (loop) networks;
- linear chains.

The practice of repatterning

How is this gestalt of perception relevant to repatterning? Practical repatterning in the individual mind or in the shared experience of group need to be based on an understanding of patterns in the mind and how they tend to be fixed (for example in belief systems) and how they can be changed. A useful starting point is the idea of the brain as a self-organising system that develops patterns according to the sequence of information it receives.

An analogy, originally attributed to Edward de Bono, is that of brain organisation as a jelly. Picture a jelly on a plate just out of its mould – a jelly mountain! From a height hot water is dripped onto the jelly and initially spatters randomly on the surface, dissolves some jelly and forms pits. After a quantity of drops has fallen subsequent drops fall into existing pits and enlarge them. Some pits, under gravity, begin to form runnels. As time passes those runnels that have become larger capture more drips and so become even larger, forming rivulets. Once this pattern is established it becomes dominant and no further pattern is likely. The sequence of drops has determined a spatial pattern.

This would appear to be a pretty insurmountable obstacle to pattern change and it does partially explain the fixity of mind-sets and belief systems. It is self-organising but in a way that is conditioned by the environment. But there is a deeper organisation possible for the brain. It is dependent on the capacity of the self to be reflexive, to exercise metacognition. More of what is being experienced in the mind needs to be taken from the tacit to the explicit. Where we are able to think about how we are thinking, to reflect on how we are reflecting or feel the way we are feeling, repatterning is possible. The analogy here shifts from a jelly to a hologram. I worked on this idea with Henri Bortoft (2012) many years ago when we both were post-graduate students of David Bohm.

Thus instead of localised parts, with the hologram the whole is present in each part and each part is distributed throughout the whole. These ideas of Bohm's encouraged some of us to think that the wholeness of human organisation, at whatever level, could not be understood adequately by means of the systems approach because something more 'holographic' was needed.

If a holographic picture is broken up just one small fragment can hold the image that is the whole picture. If one part of the mind can generate a new pattern different from the conditioned brain, it can begin to spread through the brain systems. We call it changing our mind. So the practical implication of this is that for repatterning we first need techniques to generate these 'seed' patterns and then ways to enable them to displace the previously dominant pattern.

Seven such techniques will now be described. The reader is invited to practice at least one, although experimenting with each of them gives one a much wider repertoire to tackle mental 'stuckness'. In the field you are working in to understand, solve a problem or shape a decision try these operations:

1 Forbidden combinations

Take two concepts or viewpoints that are considered by received wisdom to be contradictory, antithetical or in conflict. Write them down opposite each other on a blank sheet of paper. Hold them both in mind and ask yourself, 'How might these two actually have a positive relationship and generate some synergy?' Jot down any ideas that occur to you whilst suspending judgement as to whether they make sense.

2 Intermediate impossibles

Take an objective that you have that appears impossible. Note carefully the features of the current situation that render achieving the objective impossible. Pick one of them and think of something equally impossible that, where it achievable, would make a significant step towards the objective. Repeat this with two more features. Hold your three intermediate impossibles in mind and consider what they might be suggesting in combination.

3 Lateral imagination

Face up squarely to the situation you are in. Then, put this to one side and open some mental and emotional space. In that space let your imagination roam to a picture of a better situation, one that is initially unbelievable. Let the picture build up until you can pretend that you are in it and can feel how it is. Note some of the characteristics of being there both in the situation and in yourself.

4 Metaphorical shift

Summarise your situation, problem or decision area so you can hold it in front of your mind. Pick a natural system (tree, lion, flower etc.) and ask yourself, 'How does my situation look through this analogy? What new features of the situation does it bring out?'

5 Conceptual or axiomatic inversion

Take your situation, problem or decision and clarify within it some inherent principle or exclusion zone. State this principle clearly and then invert it. If it is 'never do this', what are the implications of doing it? If it is 'this is the only way it can work', try 'other ways can work'. If it is 'this is the most important idea', try demoting it and promoting another formerly secondary idea to be the most important. Keep making notes.

6 Experimental heuristic patterning

Sketch some diagrams of your situation – for example a pattern of items connected by lines or arranged in table. See if some symmetry suggests itself or even imposes one. Celebrate if you see things that don't fit or leave gaps. Ask yourself how might the pattern shift to feel better or what you have overlooked that might fill a gap.

7 Information sequence reversal

If your situation has a narrative that leads up to certain point, start at that point and tell the story backwards into the past. Plot the sequence in which evidence came to be gathered and then see what is suggested by feeding the evidence into your thinking in a different or reverse order.

In all of the techniques it is assumed you have been making notes. The final step is, preferably after a break, to come back to your notes with a fresh mind and see if your perspective and feeling of your original challenge has changed. Is there a new, more productive pattern emerging? Are there hints that there is more room to manoeuvre than you thought? Have these exercises clearly provoked some kind of breakthrough?

If this has worked for you, you will have confidence that getting out of 'stuckness' is possible; it is possible to change your mind and discover a new pattern of understanding. The next level of challenge is to shift this to a group working together as a collective intelligence. How can we design methods to facilitate group understanding? Is participative repatterning possible?

Participative repatterning

A point was made in Chapter 5 of the importance of the learning loop that weaves thinking and action together. However, the reflexive mutual accommodation of strategic conversation is still a rarity in management. The dominant mental orientation of managers tends to be deterministic, taking place within a power hierarchy. Management cultures are characterised by non-negotiable hierarchies and by the domination of powerful individuals who may seek advice but are often not open to reflexive review of their biases and beliefs. The result is an absence of necessary learning, a tendency to repeat previous mistakes, large-scale external diseconomies and an absence of ethical decision-making. In extreme cases this becomes pathological and has been called the 'hubris syndrome'.[2] In other words, there is an endemic incapacity to function as an effective anticipatory system.[3]

Pattern thinking requires reflexivity. Reflexivity implies that the presence of ourselves as observers is fundamental in our understanding of any situation. Reflexive participation, or from another perspective group consciousness, enhances the way groups can develop the requisite variety and shared insight for transformative innovation. Developing group consciousness requires a much more varied and articulate interface between individuals than customary meeting and communications systems allow. In design terms, the set-ups we have for group communication have very poor affordances with participative repatterning. These are some of the main requirements distilled from decades of experiment and research.

> *Ensuring inclusion for multiple perspectives*
> PRP requires procedures and facilitation to ensure all voices are heard.

> *Semantic mapping*[4]
> This breaks up the tightly linked up structure of verbal sentences and liberates meanings to become incorporated flexibly in patterns.

> *Folding thoughts together and reframing*
> The patterns need to be articulate so that they can be shifted into new configurations like a puzzle (see *idonics* later in this chapter).

Integration and synthesis
> Unlike linear documents and presentations, knowledge patterns need to be shuffled and reshuffled such that all have the option to participate in the search for new understandings.

Awareness of mental models
> This is a process of progressive elicitation since our mental models are often unconscious and need to be surfaced aided by the visual techniques and group interaction and questioning.

Assimilation to accommodation in learning[5]
> This is the process of learning originally identified by Piaget, where accommodation is the development of new schema in the mind to gain understanding which cannot be reached simply by assimilating information.

Evocation of new insights
> The important step in repatterning for both individual and group is that a new pattern of understanding and meaning is reached which was not there before the group engaged in the process.

Cognitive kinetics

These have all emerged as components of discipline we call *cognitive kinetics*. We use the term cognition rather than thinking to emphasise that we are referring to what is called enactive cognition. Cognitive kinetics (CK) is the discipline of enabling reiterative mapping of ideas (semantic units) in real time as relational patterns unfold in personal or interpersonal shared thinking and communication:

> *Cognitive*: the study of mental processes, such as 'attention, language use, memory, perception, problem solving, creativity and thinking'
> *Kinetics*: the changing patterns of relationship between of bodies (ideas) and its causes (relationships)

The process of cognitive kinetics can be summarised in four stages. First there is elicitation in which the participants are encouraged to share factors which are most significant. This is also known as a nominal group technique, which enables individuals to sort out their contribution before the dynamics of the group switches in. The second stage is gathering in, in which contributions are visually captured and visible to the group. At this stage any process to organise them into patterns is not allowed by the protocol so as to leave as many options open as possible. The third stage is synthesising, when the group work together to create new patterns of interpretation of what they have contributed, looking at relationships and emergent holistic meaning. The fourth stage is harvesting, which, as the name implies, is ensuring that the production is refined into satisfying arte-fact (usually some kind of cognitive map or model) and reflected on for personal insight as well as mutual understanding. This provides a basis for next steps in whatever the group's project is.

Effective technology and facility support for this process of cognitive kinetics require a cluster of attributers which are usually difficult to config-ure in traditional meeting spaces which have not be designed for this kind of process. They are

Visibility
   So that context and pattern can be witnessed and shared

Accessibility
   So that all involved can participate

Flexibility
   So that the kinetic reconfiguration of patterns can be represented in *real time*

Progressive build-up
   So that unfolding and emergent understanding can be created on sound foundations without loss of previous meaningful content

Ease of capture
   So that the pattern can evolve at the speed of thought and conversation

Ease of recollection when needed
   So that previous progress is not interrupted and disrupted

Human ergonomics and user handiness
   So that the process flows naturally and comfortably, not 'thrown'; important to design in these affordances

Congruence with highly interactive group procedures
   So that the tool set is able to accommodate a wide variety of tech-niques and processes consistent with the range of cognitive kinetics

Appropriate aesthetics and ambience
   So that the experience of the process is supportive and evocative to the beauty of arriving at steps of profound simplicity.

We have all become familiar with the ubiquitous yellow sticky notes used for group brainstorming. These are a more useful step than simply writing lists of ideas on flip charts, where they are virtually impossible to manipu-late. Cognitive kinetics needs a more sophisticated way of capturing and manipulating ideas than sticky notes or, indeed, the usual graphical software. The reason is the central role of the concept of idon, which is a breakthrough for participative repatterning.

Idonics – the key tool

An *idon* is defined as a *semantic unit*, that is a unit of meaning.

Idons have some specific properties which are very crucial for judgemental and creative learning. A physical idon is a moveable geometric shape. The learner/participant has freedom to place the idon in a two-dimensional space that can easily be written on by the learner/participant and easily altered or erased, as indicated in Figure 6.2.

Idons come in a variety of shapes, symbolically suited to the field of application and the thinking process. They can be colour-coded and linked by lines and arrows, which are themselves flexible and reconfigurable. Some idons, for example rectangles and hexagons, can be tiled. Tessellated patterns can be used for specific tasks in cognitive repatterning. A key use for idons is in combination with underlying frameworks that support thinking methods, sometimes referred to as problem structuring methods.

The use of idons empowers our ability to facilitate *participative complex thinking* whilst at the same time lowering the cognitive and emotional barriers to self-organised exploration of ideas, decisions, problems and holistic comprehension. It enables the *practice* of dynamic thinking to be carried out individually and in groups. Since the idon promotes the expression and clarification of a learner/participant's thinking in a visual way, it also enables the sharing of thoughts in common spaces such that similarities and differences, alternative patterns of connection and emergence of new understandings can more easily take place. This latter process is referred to as *visual dialogue*, a key thread of cognitive kinetics.[6]

Another key feature of idonic techniques is that they enable the application of cognitive structuring methods which relate to specific fields of learning and exploration. The two-dimensional substrate (whiteboard or computer

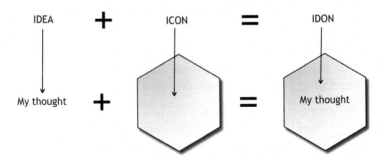

Figure 6.2 The idea of idon

screen, for instance) can depict a framework (such as a diagnostic framework or an organising concept) which brings method to the conversation. This is a prescribed component of the learning. However, the application of that concept is generated by the learners themselves with their own information, ideas and opinions such that conclusions are co-created between the learners and the conceptual framework. One example of this approach is known as problem structuring methods[7] (PSMs) used in operational research. However, it is also implicit in techniques like mind mapping. Graphical thinking and facilitation with idons is strongly based on mapping but with the additional degree of freedom that comes from being able to repeatedly move ideas around, connect them in different ways and discover new patterns of understanding.[8] In other words, idons enable kinetic processes.

Mapping has an important visual role in pattern thinking. It is a crucial way to render information and mental models visible and shareable. There are two basic forms of mapping, static and dynamic.

Static mapping provides a working patterning framework that has effectiveness backed by intellectual rigour. That framework is a basis for interrogating individual and collective thoughts captured as idons. With such maps people can make judgements as to what aspects of the map are significant. This static mapping is the basis for practical problem solving, sense making and decision-making.

Dynamic mapping take the aspects of static mapping further in a manner supportive for cognitive kinetics. It enables revision and repatterning, in real time as well as asynchronous time, in the light of new sense making, fresh perspectives, creative insight and new information. It enables participation in changing the pattern in a context of mutual exploration. In the face of hyperturbulence it facilitates the rapid generation of options through multiple recombinations in a collaborative and evolving way.

Facilitating participative repatterning

A cognitive act of recognition can be viewed as the perception of a pattern. The pattern may be a concept, a piece of writing, a picture or a scene. The key here is that the pattern is richer than, say, a reasoned argument or a stated conclusion. The pattern contains a higher variety of information and is also an indication of hidden tacit knowledge.[9]

Lists of ideas or displays of yellow tickets on a wall do not map patterns of understanding. At best they may aid some degree of basic classification but without a method and supportive tools to make the patterns manifest and to help tacit insight become explicit knowledge. This lacks coherence and power. Congruent methods of sophisticated visual representation are required. This capability is largely absent from our usual ways of working.[10]

What is needed is a discipline and medium that will support the accumulation, configuring and reconfiguring of ideas over extended time in a manner that gives as much expression to interconnections as to the ideas themselves.[11] This needs a medium of visual as well as verbal and numerical representation. A single act of recognition of a pattern is inherently static, like a snap shot of a moving scene, and the pattern is treated as having a fixed meaning, usually summarised as some kind of conclusive statement.

In solving complex problems, decision-making and designing tasks the situation is not static. There is a dynamic movement from one pattern to another, or in the evolution of a given pattern which may go through transformative changes. This needs a sequence of multiple acts of recognition which combine the known with the unknown, the determined and the emergent. Consider the dynamics of conversations that generate new ideas and insights. An idea X shared at a time t_1 may turn out to be relevant to an idea Y that emerges at t_4 but this is unknown at t_2 to t_3. Further, this relevance may be missed since the intervening conversation from t_2 to t_3 may have displaced the first idea X from memory. So the opportunity for an evolution of the pattern of understanding from the process $X + Y = Z$ is lost. For this reason, building understandings of complex patterns simply in a time linear verbal/auditory mode typical of conversation is extremely demanding on memory retention.

The use of visual recording uses space to bypass the time sequence (e.g. X and Y are written down) so that all ideas in the conversation are co-present for scanning. However, this in itself does not represent the actual patterns of connection that are in the act of recognition. So a key requirement is the facility to shift and map the patterns and connections in real time as thought is happening.

To implement cognitive kinetic process without visual mapping tools would like trying to play chess or Go! without the board and the pieces – not impossible but extremely difficult, especially to share as a collaborative process. Making meeting facilities designed for cognitive kinetics available can increase the performance of a group from the natural or habitual way people try to work together. However, facilitation procedures can be designed which further increase the effectiveness of different phases of shared thinking and problem-solving; for example, using a nominal group technique or hexagon modelling. Until a group is mutually skilled in advanced methods, a facilitator is required to achieve the best results. A deeper level of thinking requires the introduction of frameworks or mental disciplines which themselves contribute value to the process, for example dilemma modelling for the resolution of conflicts. Initially, because of the combination of a number of streams of activity, this is even more dependent on facilitation to get an effective result. Figure 6.3 shows the primary set of facilitation skills that needs to be synthesised by the practitioner to guide such processes.

Table 6.1 explains the meaning of the four components of the diagram.

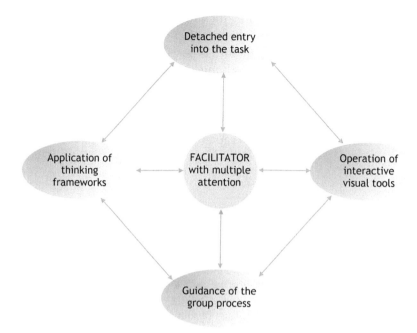

Figure 6.3 The fourfold skill set for facilitating cognitive kinetics

Table 6.1 The four primary visual facilitation skills for repatterning

Detached entry into the task	In cognitive facilitation it is important to have some grasp of the field of thinking that has been worked so that meaning can be appreciated and clarified in the idonic mapping process.
Application of thinking frameworks	Appreciation of challenge to identify the cognitive task that requires dynamic thinking. This is essential to pick conceptual frameworks that suit the needed response to the challenge.
Operation of visual tools	Easy facility with the idon tools (physical and digital) including verbal capture and geometric positioning in relation to the framework being used.
Guidance of the group process	For participative patterning it is essential to have both the procedures and the emotional skills to bring everyone into the process and steer that process through the needed stages in a flexible way.

Using these collaborative thinking and feeling methods, a group can begin to build a common APM in which they begin to function as an intelligence greater than any one of them and greater than simply the sum of the parts. An emergent holistic picture is possible. This increases the capacity to bring about transformative change in the midst of hyperturbulence rather than simply an adaptation to unexpected circumstances. Participative repatterning is at the heart of the APM and is the primary skill needed to navigate hyperturbulence. The 'ox' is ridden home. The next chapter explores some ways in which this capability can be developed.

Notes

1 Geersten, H. R. (2012). Rethinking thinking about higher-level thinking. *Teaching Sociology, 31*(1), 1–19.
2 Owen, D., & Davidson, J. (2009). Hubris syndrome: An acquired personality disorder? A study of US Presidents and UK Prime Ministers over the last 100 years. *Brain*, 1–11.
3 Fuerth, L. S., & Faber, E. M. H. (2012). *Anticipatory governance – practical upgrades : Equipping the executive branch to cope with increasing speed and complexity of major challenges.* Washington DC: Elliott School of International Affairs. Retrieved from http://forwardengagement.org/?option=com_content&view=article&id=6&Itemid=6
4 See Section 5 – Idonics – the Key Tool of CK.
5 Piaget, J. (1973). *To understand is to invent: The future of education.* Harmondsworth: Penguin Books.
6 Hodgson, A. (1992). Hexagons for systems thinking. *European Journal of System Dynamics, 59*(1), 220–230.
7 See for example Rosenhead, J. (2006). Past, present and future of problem structuring methods. *Journal of the Operational Research Society, 57*(7): 759–765.
8 Hodgson, A. (1992). Hexagons for systems thinking. *European Journal of System Dynamics, 59*(1), 220–230.
9 'Although we have known that the brain functions as a pattern processor for some time, very little work has been done to develop this area in terms of learning. Beyond the early classic works of Weinberg (1975/2001) and Bateson (1979/2002), the only emphasis in this area has been in research on categorization (Varela, Thompson, & Rosch, 1991) and more recent work in a revision of schema theory (McVee, Dunsmore, & Gavelek, 2005)'. Jeffrey W. Bloom, http://exploringsciencewiki.wikidot.com/background:patternthinking
10 *Pattern thinking* is at the core of all human thinking, in which the brain functions as a pattern recogniser (Anderson et al., 2004; Weinberg, 1975/2001). However, even with this basic functionality, much of the way we approach thinking and learning does not take full advantage of our capabilities as pattern thinkers.
11 'A fundamental operational view of pattern thinking involves a recursive approach to a loosely organized sequence of (a) recognizing patterns, (b) analyzing the functions and/or meanings of these patterns, (c) analyzing how these patterns are situated within one or more contexts, (d) finding these patterns in other contexts, and (e) using (applying, testing, analyzing, etc.) these patterns from one context in other contexts'.

Chapter 7

Transforming in the now

Step 7 – The ox out of sight, the self alone

> *The 'seeker', the 'seeking' and the 'sought' are all of the same energy
> field and therefore one and the same; the solution turns out also to
> be 'in here' not just 'out there'.*

What does our guiding ox metaphor mean for our search at this stage? I will
rephrase the traditional statement to the following: 'The system thinker, the
investigation and the system are all one energy field. Systemic capacity is
in the here and now'. If the ox represents a changed understanding of how
we need to think and view systemic aspects of the world to match the challenges of turbulence, what does it mean that this ox is 'out of sight'?

I see this as a second-order statement gone to a limit. The meaning is
that all the technical considerations point to the possibility that what is
required is not some artificial intelligence grafted onto the failing mind of

the human but an inherent potential that enables us to live at higher adaptive level quite naturally. The implication is that if we take ourselves seriously as a legitimate and even indispensable component of the system, this potential needs activating to be able to use the natural capabilities that are able to make the best use of systems thinking.

For this to work we need three bridging capabilities. First, we need to be able to be consciously present. A condition of second-order science is reflective mindfulness. Second, we need to develop latent capacities beyond the analytical rational, sometimes referred to as other ways of knowing. These capacities give us access to a greater bandwidth of information, a good deal of which is non-verbal but nonetheless practical. Third, we need to be able to hold a greater span of complexity and time in our world-view, an expanded and enriched present moment. These three capabilities will now be explored.

In the ox herding picture of Step 7 the man by his hut under the tree sits in beginner's mind and contemplates himself as a part of nature, not separate from it. For his needs he knows the ox is grazing in the meadow below, ready at his behest.

This is the seventh stage of ox herding.

~~~~~

Perception within the present moment

The acknowledgement of the presence of the observer means that his or her present moment implies that its content or 'thickness' can be at least partially known in all its multi-dimensional aspects as outlined in the description of the APM. This is not a consideration for first-order science, which makes its mainstay the production of rational causal explanation in the absence of an observer, in the sense that every observer, detached from the observation, would see the same thing, making the need to account for an observer perspective redundant. The implication is that if the present moment can be known in its richness, the rational mode of knowing on its own will not be sufficient to gain that multi-dimensional bandwidth (Hodgson, 2013). Rajagopalan[1] has proposed an extended paradigm of knowing in the field of systemic intervention. This approach can also be applied to the issue of knowing the present moment. His scheme, formulated with Midgley, draws on the work of Heron and Reason[2] (1997) in an extended epistemology. In their scheme the rational approach is only one out of four modes of

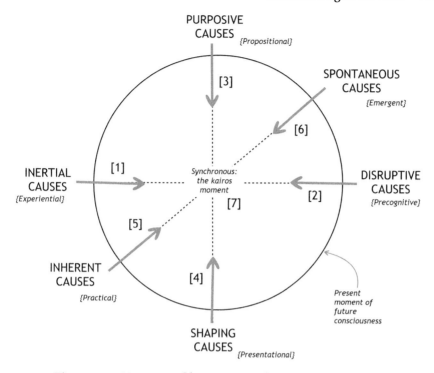

Figure 7.1 Six ways of knowing in the present moment

knowing. Figure 7.1 shows the multi-dimensional representation of the present moment.

> *Experiential* – direct immediate perception of a situation through being present in the situation. This mode of knowing is congruent with enactive perception. This gives us immediate knowledge through time corresponding to space-chronos (–).
>
> *Presentational* – essentially symbolic, expressed in aesthetic creation and design that captures and expresses meanings within the experience of the subject. In this context the observer is active and participating in a field. This corresponds to space-aionios (–).
>
> *Practical* – knowing expressed through a skill and competence and accomplishing a realisation of the meaningful content of the present moment. This corresponds to space-hyparxis (–). Although most easily recognised in the production of artefacts, it can also apply to performances and more abstract expressions, such as mathematical theories.

Propositional – knowing conceptually and descriptively depending on conventions of language and symbolism regarding a view of reality. This is the dominant way of knowing in first-order science. This corresponds to space-aionios (+).

Each of these ways of knowing access different aspects of the present moment, but this is insufficient to be open to all of the six modes of knowing that the multi-dimensional present moment implies. Rajagopalan and Midgley propose a fifth way of knowing, which they term simply 'other ways of knowing', based especially on deep practical craft knowledge.[3] In the APM this is expanded to three components, namely

Precognitive – knowing what will happen next in situations where this does not arise from historical causation alone. This is space-chronos (+).
Emergent – openness to the spontaneous and creative. It corresponds to space-hyparxis (+).
Synchronous – the seventh factor and the centre of consciousness, which makes timeless integral sense of the complex of information, impressions and intuitions.

Each way of knowing offers a perceptual window that picks up on one aspect of the present moment more strongly than another. The fundamental basis of the present moment is experience – no experience, no present moment. This experience is the complete sphere of the present moment. Propositional knowing is the basic method of first-order science based on notions of *linear causality*. Presentational knowing is the recognition and creation of *patterns*, intuitive in their source but manifest in the forms they are given. Practical knowing is the substantive *realisation* of the potential pattern in the time stream aspect of the present moment. Precognitive knowing is picking up on *retro-causal* influences. Emergent knowing is knowing what is truly possible in this present moment and *acting* to realise it.

The implications are that the capacity and effectiveness of the anticipatory present moment will partly be a function of how all forms of knowing are brought into action. This offers another practical way into realising a more potent anticipation to match the circumstances of hyper turbulence. A conscious present moment implies an openness to the richer dimensions and content through receptive presence.

Iain McGilchrist[4] has reviewed the entire field brain structure and mind function from the perspective of the asymmetry of the brain (differences in function of the left and the right hemispheres) and concludes the following:

But sequencing, in the sense of the ordering of artificially decontextualised, unrelated, momentary events, or momentary interruptions of temporal flow – the kind of thing that is as well or better performed by the left hemisphere – is not in fact a measure of the sense of time at all. It is precisely what takes over when the sense of time breaks down. Time is essentially an undivided flow: the left hemisphere tendency to break it up into units and make machines to measure it may succeed in deceiving us that it is a sequence of static points, but such a sequence never approaches the nature of time, however close it gets. This is another instance of how something that does not come into being for the left hemisphere is re-presented by in a non-living, mechanical form, the closest approximation as it sees it, but always remaining on the other side of the gulf that separates the two world – like a series of tangents that approaches ever more closely to a circle without ever actually achieving it, a machine that approximates, however well, the human mind yet has no consciousness.

In second-order science the state of mind of the observer / scientist / systems thinker is a factor in what is perceived and how it is appreciated as relevant. The mind can be compared to a radio receiver that can have extremely limited or extremely wide bandwidth. Mindfulness practices are emerging as a way to expand and 'tune-up' the mind receiver. This is well summarised by the psychiatrist Epstein.[5]

> With the mindfulness practices comes a shift from a spatially based experience of self to a temporal one. Having accomplished a certain amount of inner stability through concentration, the meditator is now able to look more closely at the moment-to-moment nature of mind and self. Mindfulness involves awareness of how constantly thoughts, feelings, images, and sensations shift in the mind and body. Rather than promoting a view of self as an entity or a place with boundaries, the mindfulness practices tend to reveal another dimension of self-experience, one that has to do with how patterns come together in a temporary and ever-evolving organization.
>
> (Epstein, 1995, p. 142)

Application of all six modes of knowing encourage a wider bandwidth of perception of the future in the present moment. However, as Rajagopalan points out, this also requires several modes of engagement with learning from experience. A range of practices, some of them very traditional, deepen our capacity for learning in each of the six modes. It also evokes the meta-cognition of which mode is in use and even increasingly being able to deliberately choose a mode to focus on to pick up more signals in the present. The facility to switch modes and pick up patterns from their interplay adds further depth.

Rajagopalan and Midgley[6] speculate on the implications this may have for improving, even rebalancing, the practice and education of systemic intervention and, I would add, for anticipatory present moment practice for foresight:

> We fear that, unwittingly, the sacredness ascribed to rational knowing in the systems community could generate strong taboos about other forms of knowing, keeping them forever on the margins of systemic intervention and thus preventing us from knowing and learning more about our world. Importantly, there is a danger here of a false evangelism masquerading as an emancipatory and participatory approach. Quite possibly, if perhaps ironically, people who possess only non-literary knowing may provide us the seeds for integration of the 'enlightened' and 'shadow' sides of our culture, at both the social and individual levels. Socially, for example, there may be clues about ways to address problems created through the dynamics of our modern economies, such as the ecological crisis; and individually, those without literacy might help to put interveners in touch with their deeper selves that they may be only dimly aware of.

Once the rejection or reluctance to explore this second-order role of the practitioner is broken, fresh methods can be explored and tested. Increasingly, research is now being gathered and codified in such relevant fields as mindfulness, creativity, precognition and even remote viewing. But the idea that these would be part of mainstream education of systems thinkers and foresight practitioners is some way off. There are still barriers as Morin points out:

> Imagination, illumination, and creation without which the progress of science would not have been possible, only entered science on the sly. They could not be logically identified, and always were epistemologically condemnable. They are spoken about in the biographies of great scientists, but never in manuals and treaties, whose sombre compilation, like subterranean layer of coal, was constituted by the fossilisation and compression what initially were fantasies, hypotheses, proliferations of ideas, inventions, and discoveries.[7]

The four modes of anticipation

The scene is now set to revisit the anticipatory present moment concept as the foundation for a practice in which systems thinking and futures thinking coalesce. Systems thinking in isolation is about a state domain and futures thinking in isolation is about a time domain. These are integrated in the APM. The distinction is made, mentioned earlier, between the 'thin' present moment and the 'thick' present moment. The former is the more or less instant now, a slice of chronological time, whereas the latter is extended in its time span by retention (distinct from memory) and protention (distinct from imagination) more richly endowed with content distributed in space and the three time-like dimensions. This structure, which was described in some detail in Chapter 4, modifies the way we interpret what we are doing when we combine systems thinking and futures thinking in active decision-making. Understanding the decision area and understanding the future are now complementary perspectives within the same focus of attention. The APM may also reflect actual neural pathways that support the anticipatory function, especially those of the right brain:

> It might be then that the division of the human brain is also the result of the need to bring two incompatible types of attention on the world at the same time, one narrow, focussed, and directed towards our needs, and the other broad, open, and directed towards whatever else is going on in the world apart from ourselves.[8]

In this case we might associate the left hemisphere with the learning from feedback from the past and the right hemisphere with the learning from the feedforward of the future.

The anticipatory present moment has a dynamic structure that integrates retention, protention, pattern, perception and anticipation. The processes of information generation from the past (feedback) make possible adaptation but not genuine anticipation. Effective anticipation requires processes of receiving information from or about the future which are not fully derivable from the past. The expanded content and dimensionality of the present moment allows for influences from the future informing our choices.

Information concerning the future which is beyond feedback adaptation is of different kinds.

1 Surrogate information on the future

This is illustrated by the creation of 'images of the future' which are dislocated from imagined futures based on trends and extrapolations, thereby introducing some new aspect that can be anticipated and affect present decisions. This explanation is favoured by those who reject any view that anticipation has features beyond linear causality.

2 *Retro-causality*

This suggests that patterns of existence unfolding over time have an ingredient of causality distinct from that coming from the past. This idea is conventionally restricted to the quantum scale world and is not considered relevant to the macro world on the scale of human affairs. However, recent research in quantum biology[9] is proposing that there are mechanisms whereby quantum effects can trigger changes that work through to the macro-behavioural level. Living beings may well have access to this kind of foreknowledge.

3 *Future consciousness*

This form of anticipation is plausible if we accept the cosmological view that the human mind is participating in a universal mind which is whole and unfragmented. This was postulated at one level by Bohm[10] as the holomovement and at another by King[11] as field of the consciousness. Since the present moment is a function of conscious self then this view accommodates a wide variety of nested present moments. In this view for a larger present moment the future of a smaller, contained present moment is already present in consciousness. What will differ is the distribution of significance in the six-dimensional continuum of space-chronos-aionios-hyparxis.

4 *Future making*

To the extent that we are creative agents we can imagine futures that have not yet come about, that would be unlikely to come about without intervention, and bring them into being. This view depends on the present moment being open and the impact of choice being beyond mechanical causality. This gets us into the knotty area of relating free will to the present moment. However, the introduction of the sixth dimension, hyparxis, is a way to accommodate the additional 'degree of freedom' needed to allow for spontaneous generation. At the human level this is the power of visualisation coupled with commitment to make something happen.

These four ways of considering anticipation at the human level are all potential capabilities in the anticipatory present moment. I say at the human level because it is emerging from more transdisciplinary review that anticipation is a universal phenomenon that operates on many levels of reality.[12] This is a field in which second-order science needs to develop a more universal perspective than the Anthropocentric.

The proposition that the present is influenced by the future is analogous to non-locality in physics – what Einstein referred to as 'spooky action at a distance'. Generally such phenomena have been discounted in mainstream science, but the accumulation of testable evidence is accumulating in a way that is beginning to soften the barrier. One recent example is the acceptance of a review paper by Cardeña[13] to a recent conference of the American Psychological Association:

> According to the first-sight model: (a) psi is not limited by the common-sensical view of time and space and is fundamental to all organisms, and (b) it mostly operates nonconsciously but may affect consciousness and action in accordance with the organism's dispositions. There are also explanations of why alterations of consciousness have been found to relate to psi. According to the 'noise reduction' theory, psi information is subtle and likely to remain nonconscious in the midst of the overwhelming information provided by the senses and bodily actions unless these inputs are reduced. Thus, procedures that reduce these stimuli – such as meditation, hypnosis, and ganzfeld – should facilitate awareness of psi. . . . Besides restriction of sensory input, alterations in consciousness may make awareness of psi more likely by reducing critical thought and stimulating a sense of interconnectedness. . . . The evidence provides cumulative support for the reality of psi, which cannot be readily explained away by the quality of the studies, fraud, selective reporting, experimental or analytical incompetence, or other frequent criticisms. The evidence for psi is comparable to that for established phenomena in psychology and other disciplines, although there is no consensual understanding of them.

A stronger view of the significance of the future is also emerging in the understanding of psychotherapy and its little explored possibilities. Seligman *et al.*[14] (2013) have proposed that we have a normal capacity to anticipate the future:

> We suggest an alternate framework in which people and intelligent animals draw on experience to update a branching array of evaluative prospects that fan out before them. Action is then selected in light of their needs and goals. The past is not a force that drives them but a resource from which they selectively extract information about the prospects they face. These prospects can include not only possibilities that have occurred before but also *possibilities that have never occurred* – and these new possibilities often play a decisive role in the selection of action.

The researches of Radin[15] suggest evidence for capacities that operate outside the boundary of conventional space-time. It may be that if we do not entertain the possibility of such capacities, we will not carry out the investigations and experiments that reveal it is a real possibility. This has already been demonstrated in his work with colleagues on remote viewing, which challenges our conventional view of the mind's relationship to space and time. Russel Targ[16] points out from his researches:

> The data from dream research like J.W. Dunne's and from remote view-ing research provide evidence that our minds have access to events occurring in distant places and to the future or past. . . . Dunne proposes an elaborate theory of 'serial time', in which our consciousness has access to time's many dimensions. This geometric approach is very much in line with physicist John Archibald Wheeler's statement that our under-standing of physics will 'come from geometry, and not from the fields.

An exercise of anticipatory consciousness

So how can this view of second-order anticipation be realised in practice? This is an open field for research. As an illustration the following section describes a couple of exercises that open up the possibilities of the six modes of future perception. It is practiced as a guided visualisation based on the dimensional structure of the present moment in Figure 7.1. The aim is to step from the con-ceptual (or propositional way of knowing) in to phenomenological approach reflecting on here-and-now experience. Each exercise takes about half an hour. The description assumes that it is being carried out in the evening.

APM exercise 1 – the stretch

1   *Collected state*

This begins from what has been called the relaxations response. Sitting comfortably but with the spine upright and head gently balanced, the aim is to come to presence, relax and free up your attention from immediate preoccupations.

2   *Presence through breathing*

Attention is given to the breathing[17] without any attempt to control the pattern. Usually there is a further natural relaxation of the breath increasing sensitive awareness. This may trigger brief yawning and natural deepening of breath, especially in the abdomen area.

3   *Visualising a memorable event from earlier in the morning*

Imagine yourself into that time location and pick one feature which is especially memorable. The more vivid that feels the more you will experience a taste of retention in the Husserlian sense where it feels different from a mere memory.

4   *Presence through breathing*

Return to the centre of the experienced present moment.

5   *Visualising a likely event tomorrow morning*

This stretches attention into the future by a few hours and links two events as one whole experience. Although imagination is used emergence there is also evoked a sense of protention, of the future being present like the past.

6   *Presence through breathing*

This again comes back to the centre of the experienced present moment. Steps 3–6 stretch the awareness of time as whole duration as well as indicating a sequence.

7   *Becoming intensely aware of this room and its contents*

This now shifts from time to space and the forms present in that space.

8   *Presence through breathing*

This comes back again to the centre of the experienced present moment.

9   *The potential of this event*

This draws attention to what is for latent for you in this 24-hour duration and might emerge from the experience. This is the latency or aionios experience.

10 *Presence through breathing*

This comes back again to the centre of the experienced present moment.

11 *A past event of significance that contributed to your interest in today*

This invites connection to a meaningful experience of the past, say, within the last two years and which is alive in the mind and has let to participating in the event.

12 *Presence through breathing*

This comes back again to the centre of the experienced present moment.

13 *To what are you drawn in the future?*

Inviting your attention to open to creative possibilities which have a feeling of attraction and even mystery. This is the hyparxis or active participation aspect of the present moment and is its strongest anticipatory aspect.

14   *Presence through breathing*

This comes back to the centre of the experienced present moment.

15   *Collected state*

Dwell in the present moment and feel how rich a single day can be. Jot down in your note book any useful observations and insights.

APM exercise 2 – reflexive questions

This exercise goes further into the six dimensions and influence on the present moment. The task is to first of all evoke them and then to reflect on how the signals you receive might change the way you see the world and hence what you will privilege as anticipatory actions. The exercise is constructed around the following model.

You begin by picking an area of the future you are especially interested in. It might be sustainability, or social well-being or political change, for example. You need to choose a time span. Suggested time spans would be from five to fifteen years from now making the present moment ten to thirty years.

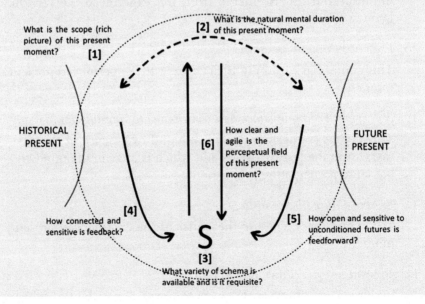

Phase 1 – What are your initial speculative thoughts looking x years ahead?

Phase 2 – Reflect on and answer the seven anticipatory questions based on the model.

Phase 3 – Reflect on comparing the output of Phase 2 with the initial picture of Phase 1.

You will find creating a table, such as the following, quite helpful to capture your thoughts. They may occur in any order – although start off by going through them one at a time.

QUESTION	YOUR THOUGHTS
1 *What is likely to come about by momentum from the past?*	
2 *What seems to be new **not** coming from the past?*	
3 *What is a positive potential beyond these events?*	
4 *What tangible forms are likely to dominate?*	
5 *What has the most promising life in it for the future?*	
6 *Can you see/sense/imagine a desirable outcome that would be surprising?*	
7 *What now is the essential value of this future in the present moment?*	

Some generic reflections that can emerge are: 'maybe our ways of designing the future are based too much on fear of failure rather than freedom of success', 'acknowledging the subject – how to do that in a mindful way', 'how does the future influence the present', 'it enriched my picture', 'fleeting images with my children in them', 'appreciating the time span'.

Tapping our potential

I believe this 'new' form of systemic consciousness is actually already latent within the human being. What principally prevents its release and realisation is the domination of incongruent cultural and academic conditioning and world-view propaganda. So in spite of the complications of trying to unravel this, the primary requirement is simply there if we can tap into it.

Embedded in this challenge are a number of dilemmas.[18] By a dilemma[19] I mean a pair of seemingly opposite and incompatible factors that, without creative resolution, are mutually exclusive. They seem impossible to live together in the same space and time. It is the reconciliation of these contradictions which is the clue to the change in systems thinking needed to match its capability to the hyperturbulent environment.

> We need to think more clearly about the future and improve our anticipatory skills. AND
> We need to be much quicker in our actions and reactions to navigate the turbulence.

> We need to be much more objective about the mismatch of our understandings, including the scientific, with the way the world actually works. AND
> We need to reincorporate the subjective into the way we see and understand the world if we are to understand its holistic properties.

> We need a culture which releases and respects both the creativity and the capacity for ethical choice of the individual. AND
> We need a culture which privileges the skills and capacities of groups to co-create both better systems of adaptation and resilience and community coherence.

To attempt the resolution of these dilemmas, we now have the ingredients for a fresh perspective in considering what is needed to navigate in a hyperturbulent world. In summary:

First, we need to rehabilitee the observer and boldly create a more generalised approach to second-order systems science, drawing on building on disciplines like second-order cybernetics, action research and anthropology.

Second, through the second-order paradigm we need to integrate future thinking with systems thinking so that we can deal recursively with multiple scales and time-frames. In Chapter 3, I proposed the three horizons method as a powerful way to handle three perspectives on time and the future and multiple scales from individuals to large strategic programmes. This has special reference to enabling us to frame transformation rather than just change. Transformation is important because enhancing the current paradigm is not going to get us where we need to be.

Third, we need to recognise that the way we design systems in practice almost completely depends on feedback as the adaptive principle, whereas turbulence challenges us to anticipate that which has not yet happened, especially that which cannot be simply inferred from past and present evidence. We need to recognise that anticipatory systems are possible, but they have a property, usually hidden from sight, of feedforward. This means they have a means of perceiving the 'not yet'. This functionality is mumbo-jumbo unless we question the basis of what we mean by time and extend beyond our current mechanistic view of time. In this way we leave room to explore alternative ways of knowing which are properties especially of living things and of consciousness.

Fourth, and following from the last point, we need to reperceive the nature of time, the future and pattern. In Chapter 4 this is developed as the concept of the anticipatory present moment, where the signals that may influence decisions about the future are coming from several dimensions. This view is essentially phenomenological and deeply depends on the presence of sentient consciousness in the decision-maker.

From this perspective the nature of decision-making and its ethical implications can be developed in a new way around the notion of 'undecidable questions'. I call this *decision integrity*, in which systems thinking is integrated with wisdom and ethics. A key here is the principle that ethical choices emerge from and are the requirement when faced with such undecidable questions, a notion that does not sit comfortably for a those with the world-view that all is reducible to AI algorithms. Such questions are a fundamental property of turbulent situations. In a fragmented and dissociated world such ethics is programmed out and the issue is largely avoided. This is the fifth ingredient.

The sixth ingredient is the recognition, from cybernetics, that our ways of functioning in society and making decisions lacks the requisite variety, quantitatively and qualitatively, and that neither 'big brains' nor smart organisations can meet this requirement in a turbulent society. In Chapter 6 the process of people cooperating and cocreating in a shared consciousness is explored. This is illustrated by some practical methods which harness visual thinking to augment verbal and mathematical thinking. It highlights that the kind of systems thinking we now need to develop is inseparable from the development of artful and effective facilitation.

The key to the resolution we seek lies in recognising the immense richness of a deeper appreciation of what I call *the now*. To gain that appreciation and set the scene for new practices of systems thinking, decision-making and responsiveness, it is necessary to dig into the difficult area of the nature of time itself. Our misconceptions and inability to understand time itself have led to deeply ingrained assumptions about what we are doing and why in terms of our practical affairs. Unearthing these assumptions and entertaining different ones gets to the heart of how we experience or fail to experience life and what practices we can cultivate to rectify this.

Coming to grips with *the now*

To get to grips with *the now*, we need to get beyond the simplistic division of time into past, present and future and our failure to recognise that our actual experience is in some way tenseless.[20] It is all taking place *now*. This now is much richer in its dimensions and its context than we usually attribute. This richer form of *the now* we call the *present moment*.

So we now need to understand how far the past-present-future distinction can be contained within the present moment. An event which has 'immediately passed' is still experienced and therefore not simply memory, and an event 'just coming-to-be' is also experienced and not simply a prediction. This can be seen as a filling out of a 'thick' present moment. Our experience of time as temporal extension and duration is not built up from awareness of succession but rather from an awareness of succession derived from a direct awareness of a 'whole time' already experienced.

The present moment is a property of a self, a subjective experience. We can connect the idea of the present moment with the concept of second-order cybernetics. First-order cybernetics is essentially reductionist and follows the implicit rule that the observer does not enter into the observation. However, the present moment is where we experience life. To have any direct perception and sure knowledge, this present moment is all that there is. From a second-order perspective the observer and observation are inseparable and the act of observation must take place in someone's present moment.

This present moment is constantly changing, a state of 'perpetual perishing' which we interpret as linear time. However, it is also in a state of 'perpetual renewal', sustaining the here and now. Its variations for each one of us is a function of our own consciousness in the present.[21]

A disjunction between our experience of the present moment and the whole interpretive edifice that we have constructed around time, stasis and change reveals the subjectivity of objectivity. We live a continuous present for which, as observers, we invent pasts, presents and futures to give account of now.[22] In this sense the present moment can itself be considered a way of languaging our reflections on being present in this living moment and as an aspect of the continuous process of creating ourselves as self-generating beings[23]

Notes

1 Rajagopalan, R., & Midgley, G. (2015). Knowing differently in systemic intervention. *Systems Research and Behavioral Science, 32*, 546–561.
2 Heron, J., & Reason, P. (1997). A participatory enquiry paradigm. *Qualitative Inquiry, 3*(3), 274–294.
3 Rajagopalan & Midgley, Knowing differently in systemic intervention.
4 McGilchrist, I. (2009). *The master and his emissary: The divided brain and the making of the western world*. New Haven: Yale University Press. p. 76.
5 Epstein, M. (1995). *Thoughts without a thinker: Psychotherapy from a Buddhist perspective*. New York: Basic Books.
6 Rajagopalan & Midgley, Knowing differently in systemic intervention, p. 559.
7 Morin, E. (2008). *On complexity*. Cresskill, NJ: Hamilton Press. p. 34.
8 McGilchrist, *The master and his emissary*, p. 27.
9 Al-Khalili, J., & McFadden, J. (2014). *Life on the edge: The coming of age of quantum biology*. London: Bantam Press.
10 Bohm, D., & Nichol, L. (Ed.). (2003). Super-implicate order. In *The essential David Bohm*. Abingdon: Routledge.
11 King, C. (2014). *Space, time and consciousness*. Retrieved from www.dhushara.com/stc/ct.pd
12 Poli, R. (2010). The many aspects of anticipation. *Foresight, 12*(3), 7–17.
13 Cardeña, E. (2018). The experimental evidence for parapsychological phenomena: A review. *American Psychologist, 73*(5), 663–677.
14 Seligman, M. E. P., Railton, P., Baumeister, R. F., & Sripada, C. (2013). Navigating into the future or driven by the past. *Perspectives on Psychological Science, 8*, 119.
15 Radin, D. (2006). *Entangled minds: Extrasensory experiences in a quantum reality*. New York: Paraview Pocket Books.
16 Targ in Dunne, J. W. (2001). *An experiment with time* (Preface by Russell Targ). Charlottesville: Hampton Roads. p. ix.
17 'The simple discipline of concentration brings us back to the present moment and all the richness of experience that it contains. It is a way to develop mindfulness, the faculty of alert and sensitive awareness'. Retrieved October 16, 2015, from https://thebuddhistcentre.com/text/mindfulness-breathing
18 The nature of dilemmas is explained in Chapter 8.
19 Hampden-Turner, C. (1990). *Charting the corporate mind: From dilemma to strategy*. Oxford: Blackwell.
20 In his analysis of this from a philosophical perspective, Mozersky (2006, p. 441) asserts that there are no elemental properties that distinguish past, present or future. He goes on to affirm that from the perspective of conscious experience there are two aspects we need to consider. 'First, the present is experientially privileged in that we are only ever capable of experiencing that which occurs in the present. . . . Secondly, as we interact with the world it appears as if time, in some non-metaphorical sense, passes; what was future becomes present and then passes'.
21 'The extent and coherence of the present moment are evidently connected with the embrace of our awareness. We can say the present moment of each one of us is relative to the integrative power of our own will. For subjective idealism, the present moment is nothing but the content of the mind. For objective materialism, the mind is nothing but the context of the present moment. The two viewpoints are contradictory only if we import artificial distinctions of past, present and future, or here and now, there or elsewhere, into our interpretations of experience' Bennett (1966, p. 14).

22 'We live our existing in language as if language were a symbolic system for referring
to entities of different kinds that exist independently from what we do, and we treat
even ourselves as if we existed outside language as independent entities that use language. Time, matter, energy, . . . would be some of those entities' Maturana (1995, p. 2).

23 'our existing in language as if language were a symbolic system for referring to
entities of different kinds that exist independently from what we do, and we treat
even ourselves as if we existed outside language as independent entities that use
language. Time, matter, energy, . . . would be some of those entities'. Maturana, H.
R. (1995). The nature of time. *Instituto de Terapia Cognitivia, Santiago de Chile.*
Retrieved from www.inteco.cl/biology/nature.htm. p. 2.

Chapter 8

Natural systems thinking

Step 8 – Entering the market place with helping hands

The search for the ox has now transcended the ox with a new understanding which discovers that what is difficult for us is the limitations of our conventional world-views, whereas a natural appreciation of our lived experience is at the root of transformational action.

Going back to Figure 1.1 showing the systemic role of world-view, we can now ask if the APM is a better position from which to switch from the accelerating mismatch of human life to its planetary environment to a positive regeneration of life cultures that enhance humanity and nature. Daniel Wahl (2016) puts the challenge succinctly:

> In the end it comes down to asking ourselves: will we continue to strive to outcompete each other and in the process unravel the thread that

all life depends upon? Or will we learn to collaborate in the healing of the whole through transformative innovation and regenerative design creating vibrant cultures and thriving communities for all?

It takes working with a considerable and focused effort to affirm a change of consciousness and its associated rewiring of our brains and nervous system. The gap between our intentions and our actions reveals this. The good news is that if internalisation really takes place, a change in action and behaviour comes naturally. The seeds of regenerative ideas will sprout in some practical form.

The seeker for a new paradigm discovers that this paradigm is already inherent in his or her being but now has a language and road-map for its development. Second-order awareness and reflection create the basis of double-loop learning, in which the patterns which determine our action and our judgements change how we understand a situation, how we understand ourselves in that situation and what is the most systemic and holistic action we can take.

The new paradigm is being discovered through a metamorphic sequence of the breakdown of the validity of the status quo, the experience of being lost and of seeking the new and discovering the mental equivalent of imaginal cells and the increasing reorganising power of these imaginal cells to form and reform the pattern – from caterpillar to chrysalis to butterfly. Then, our practice and interventions, on their own scale, spread helpful shifts in the way we influence and change the game of life in as natural a way as possible. Truly, human intelligence outsmarts artificial intelligence since the latter can only be based on knowledge from the past, which is the dehumanising paradigm. AI might be programmed to be moral, but it will not be able to deal with the escalating situations of undecidable questions as discussed in Chapter 5.

The emerging capacity to live well in the face of hyperturbulence becomes contagious.

This is the eighth stage of ox herding.

~~~~~

Systems thinking as qualitative practice

Over the last fifty years, systems thinking has come a long way. However, of the two components, the systems component part has developed way ahead of the thinking component. This imbalance has caused a lop-sided development in which the emphasis has been on systems as a technical field of modelling and mathematics and following from that the application of tools and techniques very much in the paradigm of first-order science.

This has been at the expense of the development of the thinking component. There are several reasons for this, many of them cultural, such as the domination of specialisation in academia and the domination of functional hierarchies in organisations. Here I want to concentrate on the personal psychological issues that seem to restrict the potential of systems thinking as a skill and capacity much needed to be developed and adopted in the world of hyperturbulence.

The core issue from the investigations by myself and my colleagues is our failure to appreciate the nature of wholeness and the role that qualities play in structured processes, whether external to ourselves or internal to our perceptions. Further, we treat these two aspects as separate rather than as a seamless participation in the world process through our consciousness. Without the sense of wholeness, we fail to cultivate the perceptions and skills to navigate the hyperturbulent world. Fundamental to understanding this view of understanding is the appreciation of the relationship between structure and process.

We can investigate this through looking at the nature of order in a way that falls neither into the trap of having some absolute external reference as to reality nor into the trap of absence of regularity and disconnection from any kind of order. The key lies in perhaps the most fundamental notion of systems thinking, the interrelationship between structure and process. This is portrayed in Figure 8.1 as a mutual loop which forms a continuous

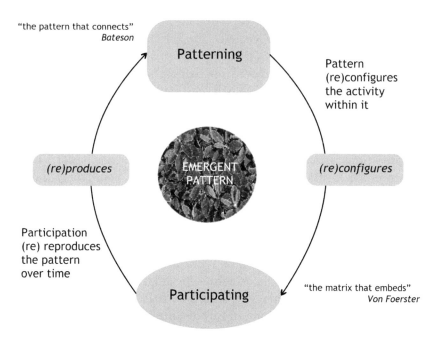

Figure 8.1 Systemic reality as a recurrent participative process (Sharpe)

recurrence. The pattern that connects expresses the lives that embody that generate the pattern that connects.

The first-order version of this is evident in the general processes of life without the presence of self-awareness. The second-order version introduces the power to reflect on the patterning and thereby *gain the freedom to change the pattern*. The first is a process to sustain dominant patterns that can only be broken by external force or accident, whereas the second enables the entry of creative and ethical values in the reconstruction of patterns. This view combines Gregory Bateson's insight into 'the pattern that connects' with Heinz von Foerster's 'matrix that embodies' and Varela's notion of enactive cognition where neither representation nor mechanism alone explains knowing.

A fundamental dilemma of systems thinking

A way of going deeper into the nature of structure-process is to treat the pair as a dilemma. This way of understanding the cybernetics of seeming polarities which at a deeper level are complementarities is attributable to Charles Hampden-Turner, who was an early student of Gregory Bateson and his double-bind theory. The systemic structure of a dilemma is that there are two equally necessary and desirable values and objectives that have apparently irreconcilable and contradictory characteristics that propel them into what appear as either/or choices. However, if only one is chosen, the absence of the other leads to failure. In a dilemma there is a deeper structural coupling that is cybernetic. The rejected value will come back and bite!

The consequence is that if we concentrate wholly on systems as an external property of the world, we will increasingly become divorced from our presence in their applications. On the other hand, if we concentrate exclusively on the reflecting and philosophising, we will become divorced from meaningful practice. Yet the resolution of this tension is not so easy. It requires transformative innovation, which in turn needs participative repatterning. In a hyperturbulent world that needs *continuous* transformative innovation rather than a 'one off' solution. Transformative innovation must be continuously generated. So we talk about navigating our way through the dilemma space.

In this book I have proposed a development of systems thinking that integrates the objectivity of systems with the subjectivity of thinking in a way that avoids splitting the dilemma by migrating the systems paradigm to be second order. This is enhanced by realising that navigating the dilemma requires the integration of futures thinking.

The dilemma space represented in Figure 8.2 gives us a way to map systems approaches in relation to the way they play out in the dynamics of this

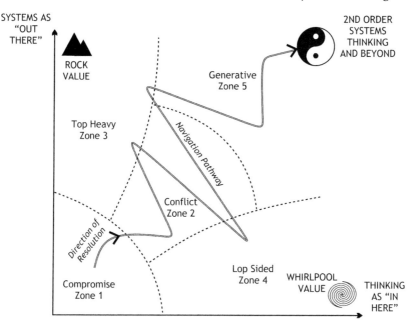

Figure 8.2 The dilemma space

dilemma space. This useful symbology was developed by Charles Hampden-Turner and draws on Greek mythology, namely navigating between the rock (the 'hard objective' value) and the whirlpool (the 'soft subjective' value).

On the vertical rock axis is placed *systems as 'out there'*. These are the various disciplines of systems science that take the observer for granted. They tend towards 'systems are real'. On the horizontal whirlpool axis is placed *thinking as 'in here'*. These are the various philosophies that question the reality of systems and see them as useful but arbitrary distinctions that we have subjectively made. The resolution zone, *second-order systems thinking and beyond*, is an indication that there is a third space possible that not only integrates the two apparently incompatible positions but also points towards a new emergent discipline.

The orthogonal axis presents not an opposition but a distinction that creates a two-dimensional space which can be divided into five zones with fuzzy boundaries. Four of these zones represent failure or incompleteness to navigate or resolve the dilemma successfully. The fifth zone is successful in balancing the tension without losing the force and integrity of both values.

Zone 1 is the compromise area where the tension is swept under the carpet and ignored as if it will go away. This leads inevitably to degradation. Zone 2 is the conflict zone where the two positions are arguing on a

Table 8.1 Systems methods and their relationship to the
systems thinking dilemma

Zone 1	– vague reference to the 'systems thing' need for 'whole systems' but no technical knowledge and no reflective thinking on meaning; artificial intelligence (intelligence without humanity); control and management systems
Zone 2	– the war between hard and soft systems thinking, AI versus human insight, conflicting systems world-views
Zone 3	– system dynamics modelling, VSM, generic algorithms, artificial intelligence
Zone 4	– soft systems modelling, critical systems
Zone 5	– systemic intervention (Midgley, 2000), boundary critique (Ulrich, 1983), DSIP (Cabrera & Cabrera, 2015), systems holism (Jackson, 2003), the 'Fifth Discipline' (Senge, 1990), regenerative cultures (Wahl, 2016), world system model (Hodgson, 2011), '21st CC' (Leicester & O'Hara, 2009), 'Theory U' (Scharmer, 2009), 'Value Creating Systems' (Ramirez & Mannervic, 2016), action research (Bradbury, 2015)

polarised 'I'm right; you're wrong' basis. This breeds confusion and wasted resources. Zone 3 we call 'top-heavy'. The systems view dominates from within the first-order reductionist paradigm. Zone 4 we call 'lop-sided'. The view is that systems are purely mental models of pragmatic value but do not correspond to anything real. In Zone 5 there is the possibility of resolution. However, since the tension is dynamic, such a resolution is bound to be temporary. The power and value of a conscious dilemma is that it creates an ongoing generative space. It is a continuously evolving story.

Having created the dilemma space and its meaning, we can take a more nuanced discrimination between modes of systems thinking by seeing roughly where their centre of gravity lies in the dilemma space. Some illustrative examples are shown in Table 8.1. These are very rough indications because often methods are spread out across the dilemma space.

Systems knowledge; systems understanding

Understanding is a function of the whole person participating in the whole system. Knowledge is not the same as the content: it is in some way objectified and codified. No amount of knowledge in itself will lead to understanding, because the person is not present to be that understanding. Understanding requires a conscious reflection that is aware of the topic of understanding and the experience of understanding. It is of the essence of the second-order paradigm. This viewpoint will raise the criticism that understanding is entirely subjective and cannot be a cultural artefact like knowledge and language.

To understand that this is not the case, we need to appreciate the full cycle of the relationship between understanding and knowledge. A useful insight into this is developed here from the concept of the i-space developed by Max Boisot. This is summarised in the diagram Figure 8.3.

Understanding is personal, concrete and tacit. In that sense it is uncodified. In attempting to formulate and communicate understanding codification is developed into some appropriate language which may be verbal, visual or mathematical. At this stage some knowledge is extracted from the original understanding and can therefore be diffused and become 'social property'. As such it then becomes part of the cultural background and carries with it not just the extracted knowledge but also the implicit values or world-view of the originator. Both the knowledge and the culture are coloured by this. Repatterning involves the origination of new tacit understanding which then must go through its own codification and diffusion process to displace the preceding 'normalcy'.

This cycle can then operate further in two ways. In one way a person questions the knowledge and its cultural assumptions and starts a new cycle with new tacit understandings. In the other way, a person picks up the knowledge from being in the culture and traces it back to its origins

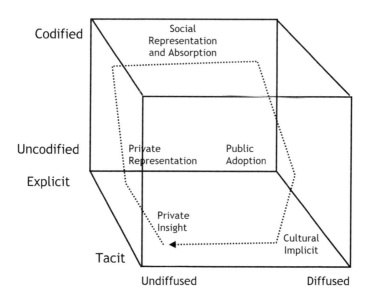

Figure 8.3 Paradigm shift in the Boisot i-space

in order to understand it better. In this way understanding and knowing are seen as aspects of a systemic cycle of intelligence of unbroken wholeness. If this cycle is not appreciated, either consciously or instinctively, then fragmentation between personal consciousness and knowledge takes place. From this flows the imbalance, misalignment and ethical harm that flow from the unconscious application of technology, including systems science.

One of the characteristics of reflective understanding for repatterning is that the observer is accommodated and qualities are appreciated. Referring back to the recognition of wholeness as being fundamental to the systems approach, we can now open up the importance of recognising the nature of systems not just from their behaviour but also in terms of their perceivable but non-measurable qualities. We can also now position the observer as a key to the perception of qualities which are not accessible to measurement in the absence of human consciousness, however clever artificial intelligence simulations might be.

In the introduction of this book I outlined as a metaphor of my investigation the stages of spiritual ox herding from the Zen tradition. It seems to me after decades of research and practice that there is a universal wisdom in this story for any exploration, scientific or artistic, into an unknown region. Reaching the conclusion of this particular journey (there are many others to be made) let's look back and retrace the steps.

Step 1 – Seeking the ox
Things are not working and provoke a search for something better – enhancing systems thinking opening the space between systems and thinking.

Step 2 – Finding the tracks
An approach is discovered – namely including the observer as legitimate creating opportunity to consider the benefit of additional ways of knowing.

Step 3 – First glimpse of the ox
A promising clue is found – understanding of the future needs to be reframed stepping out of limited interpretations of time that are closing down our range of perceptions.

Step 4 – Catching the ox
Now another view of system is possible – upframing the significance of anticipatory *systems* recognizing that the future is active and not simply a product of the ongoing past.

Step 5 – Taming the ox
The meaning of decision is changed – harmonisation of inner and outer through integrity in the face of the undecidable questions of turbulence.

Step 6 – Riding the ox home
The insights illuminate collective intelligence – the application of participative repatterning as a collaborative enhancement of individual capacity essential for the emerging Anthropocene.

Step 7 – The ox out of sight, the self alone
The realisation of wholeness – all is now in the present moment of the system which includes us encouraging us to find the source of systemic understanding in ourselves as well as in formal disciplines.

Step 8 – Entering the market place with helping hands
Self and source united – we can release the systemic capacities we need because they are latent and called for in great measure to engage creatively with the global imperatives of our age.

Chapter 1 began with the proposition that our fragmented world needs healing. Healing is a deeper process than fixing. Our first-order techno-culture is remarkable in its power to fix things but suffers enormously from the systemic property of unintended consequences. It also suffers from the hijacking of technological capability for satisfaction of ambition and greed that are inherently unhealthy and destructive of human and planetary well-being. A shift to a second-order understanding of the nature of the world and our relationship with it is one, out of many, transformative changes that could move us from an explosion of 'fixes that fail' to a counter trend of ethical wholeness where responsibility for the mess cannot so easily be 'juggled away'.

Bibliography

Ackoff, R. (1981). *Creating the corporate future*. Chichester: Wiley.

Albrow, M. (1997). *The global age*. Stanford: Stanford University Press.

Argyris, C. (1990). *Overcoming organizational defenses, facilitating organizational learning*. Boston: Allyn and Bacon.

Argyris, C., & Schon, D. (1978). *Organisational learning*. Reading, MA: Addison Wesley.

Bateson, G. (1972). *Steps towards an ecology of mind*. Chicago: Chicago University Press.

Beer, S. (1994). *Beyond dispute: The invention of team syntegrity*. Chichester: Wiley.

Bennett, J. G. (1966). *The dramatic universe* (Vols. 1–4, Vol. 1). London: Hodder and Stoughton.

Bohm, D., & Hiley, B. (1993). *The undivided universe*. London & New York: Routledge.

Bohm, D., & Nichol, L. (Ed.). (2003). *The essential David Bohm*. London: Routledge. p. 193.

Bortoft, H. (2012). *Taking appearance seriously: The dynamic way of seeing in Goethe and European thought*. Edinburgh: Floris Books. p. 13.

Bradbury, H., (2015). *The SAGE Handbook of Action Research*. London: Sage Publications.

Cabrera, D., & Cabrera, L. (2015). *Systems thinking made simple: New hope for solving wicked problems*. Odyssean Press.

Clemson, B. (1984). *Cybernetics: A new management tool*. Tunbridge Wells, England: Abacus Press.

Cullender, C. (2014). Is time an illusion? *Scientific American, 23*(4), 14–21.

Davies, P. (2019). *Demon in the machine: How hidden webs of information are solving the mystery of life*. London: Allen Lane.

de Geus, A. (1988). Planning as learning. *Harvard Business Review* (March-April), 70–74. Reprint Berg.

Epstein, M. (1995). *Thoughts without a thinker: Psychotherapy from a Buddhist perspective*. New York: Basic Books.

Gell, A. (1992). *The anthropology of time: Cultural constructions of temporal maps and images*. Oxford: Berg.

Goodman, P. S. (1966). *An empirical examination of Elliott Jaques' concept of Time Span'*. Tepper School of Business, Carnegie Mellon University. Retrieved from http://repository.cmu.edu/tepper

Hampden-Turner, C. (1990). *Charting the corporate mind: From dilemma to strategy*. Oxford: Blackwell.

Hodgson, A. (2011). *Ready for anything: Designing resilience for a transforming world*. Axminster: Triarchy Press.

Hodgson, A. (2013). Towards an ontology of the present moment. *On the Horizon, 21*(1), 24–38.

Hodgson, A. (2016). *Time, pattern, perception: Integrating systems and futures thinking* (PhD thesis). University of Hull. Retrieved from www.academia.edu.

Hodgson, A. (2017). Reperceiving the future. *World Futures Review, 9*(4), 208–224.

Hodgson, A. (2018). Second order anticipatory systems. In R. Poli (Ed.), *Handbook of anticipation*. New York: Springer.

Holland, J., Holyoak, K., Nisbett, R., & Thagard, P. (1986). *Induction: Processes of inference, learning and discovery*. Cambridge, MA: MIT Press.

Jackson, M. (2003). *Systems thinking: Creative holism for managers*. Chichester: Wiley.

Koestler, A. (1967). *The ghost in the machine*. London: Hutchinson.

Kurtzweil, R. (1990). *The age of intelligent machines*. Cambridge, MA: MIT Press.

Leicester, G. (2016). *Transformative innovation: A guide to practice and policy*. Axminster: Triarchy Press.

Leicester, G., & O'Hara, M. (2009). *Ten things to do in a conceptual emergency*. Aberdour, Scotland: IFF/Triarchy.

Lombardo, T. (2006). *The evolution of future consciousness*. Bloomington, IN: AuthorHouse.

Markley, O. (2012). Imaginal visioning for prophetic foresight. *Journal of Future Studies, 17*(1), 5–24.

Maturana, H. R., & Varela, F. J. (1987). *The tree of knowledge: The biological roots of human understanding*. Boston & London: Shambhala.

McCann, J. E., & Selsky, J. (1984). Hyperturbulence and emergence of type 5 environments. *The Academy of Management Review, 9*(3), 460–470.

Midgley, G. (2000). *Systemic intervention; philosophy, methodology, and practice*. New York: Kluwer.

Morecroft, J. (2007). *Strategic modelling and business dynamics*. Chichester, UK: Wiley.

Morin, E. (1999). *Seven complex lessons in education for the future*. Paris: UNESCO.

Morin, E. (2008). *On complexity*. Cresskill, NJ: Hamilton Press.

Morin, E. (in press). *Confronting complexity*. A. Heath-Carpentier (Ed.). Albany: SUNY Press.

Müller, K., Flanagan, T., Midgley, G., Wahl, D., Hämäläinen, T., Lähteenmäki-Smith, K., . . . Getz, L. (2017). Second order science and policy. *World Futures, 73*.

Muller, K. H. (2016). *Second-order science: The revolution of scientific structures*. Wien: Edition Echoraum. p. 37.

Novotny, H. (1994). *Time: The modern and postmodern experience*. Cambridge: Polity Press.

O'Hara, M., & Leicester, G. (2012). *Dancing on the edge: Competence, culture and organization in the 21st century*. Axminster: Triarchy Press.

Poli, R. (2010). The many aspects of anticipation. *Foresight, 12*(3), 7–17.

Poli, R. (Ed.). (2018). *Handbook of anticipation*. New York: Springer.

Ramage, M., & Shipp, K. (Eds.). (2009). *Systems thinkers*. London: Springer.

Ramanan, K. V. (1966). *Nagarjuna's philosophy*. New York: Samuel Weiser.

Ramirez, R, & Mannervic, U. (2016). *Strategy for a networked world*. London: Imperial College Press.

Rosen, R. (1985). *Anticipatory systems: Philosophical, mathematical and methodological foundations*. Oxford: Pergamon Press.

Rosenhead, J. (2006). Past, present and future of problem structuring methods. *The Journal of the Operational Research Society, 57*(7): 759–765.

Scharmer, C. O. (2009). *Theory U: Leading from the future as it emerges*. Oakland: Berrett-Koehler Publishers.

Senge, P. (1990). *The fifth discipline: The art and practice of the learning organization*. New York: Doubleday/Currency.

Sharpe, B. (2013). *Three horizons: The patterning of hope.* Axminster: Triarchy Press.

Sharpe, B., Fazey, L., Hodgson, A., Leicester, G., & Lyon, A. (2016). Three horizons: A pathways practice for transformation. *Ecology and Society 21*(2), 47.

Sharpe, B., & van de Heijden, K. (2007). *Scenarios for success: Turning insights into action.* Chichester, England: John Wiley & Sons Ltd.

Steffen, W, Richardson, K., Rockström, J., Cornell, S.E., Fetzer, I., Bennett, E. M., . . . Sörlin, S. (2015). Planetary boundaries: Guiding human development on a changing planet. *Science, 347*(6223). doi:10.1126/science.1259855.

Sterman, J. (2000). *Business dynamics: Thinking and modeling for a complex world.* Boston: Irwin McGraw-Hill.

Ulrich, W. (1983). *Critical heuristics of social planning: A new approach to practical philosophy.* Bern: Haupt.

van de Heijden, K. (2005). *Scenario planning: The art of strategic conversation.* Chichester, England: John Wiley & Sons Ltd.

Varela, F., Thompson, E., & Rosch, E. (1991). *The embodied mind.* Cambridge, MA: MIT Press.

von Foerster, H. (2014). *The beginning of heaven and Earth has no name* (A. Muller & K. H. Muller, Eds.). New York: Fordham University Press.

Wahl, D. C. (2016). *Designing regenerative cultures.* Axminster: Triarchy Press.

Index